Holy Chutzpah!
Snapshots of Everyday Faith

Gerrie Hyman Mills
with Cynthia Cutts

Gerrie Hymn Mills

Gerrie Hymn Mills

.

Gerrie Hymn Mills

TABLE OF CONTENTS

Chapter		Page
	Acknowledgement	10
1	What is Chutzpah?	11
2	Praying for Palms	18
3	Growing Up Jewish	22
4	Jewish Daughter, Christian Wife	26
5	Early Married Years	34
6	Called to Ministry	38
7	The Red Negligee	42
8	A Big Surprise	47
9	Lost or Left Behind	50
10	Pretty Little Blonde Hero	55
11	Then Came Grant	69
12	A Child's Prayer	74
13	Adapting to the Situation: My short-lived career as an athlete	77
14	The Short Cut Fight	82

15 Grow a Notch in Faith   89

16 Conspiracy   93

17 Grandpa's Homecoming   97
    Queen

18 Miracle in a Concert Hall   107

19 Colleen and the Red Eye Flight   111
    that Changed her Life

20 Keys in the Ocean   118

21 Mirror, Mirror on the Wall   122

22 I Can't Hear You   129

23 Lost at Sea   135

24 Holy Nudges   140

25 Reggie   145

26 The Survivor   150

27 Strangers in the Holy Land   156

28 Close Call on the Highway   159

29 String Cheese at Costco   162

30 My Seventy-fifth Birthday   169

31	An Unexpected Christmas Blessing	175
32	Faith in Business	179
33	If Not Now, When?	183
34	Behind Every Successful Pastor, There is a Wife Praying	190
35	We Plan - God Laughs	195
36	Family Legacy	202
37	My Jewish Roots Run Deep	222
	Clyde	233
	From The Editor (Friend)	237

Gerrie Hyman Mills

DEDICATION

To my daughter and daughter-in-loves, Lori Anne, Ellen, Cathy and Michelle — you are my best friends — steady in faith, unconditional in love, strong in character, and faithful in text messaging.

Luv u 4,
Mom

ACKNOWLEDGEMENT

I'm grateful to my family for giving me such an incredible subject matter to write about. They are one fun and exciting bunch! I feel so blessed! And, after helping me through all of these months of compiling the content of this book, they actually still love me. Now that's true love! A special thanks to Lori and David for their countless hours of hard work and creativity and to Clyde for his encouragement, love and support.

To Fizzy Edwards, Bradley Simkins, Patricia Hake, Cindy Cutts, Karen Pascoe and her daughter-in-law, Kayla, I've enjoyed a fruitful relationship with each of you and words just can't describe how much I appreciate your contribution.

SNAPSHOT 1

What is Chutzpah?

My Jewish roots grow deeply. I grew up in Michigan, surrounded by a lively, loud Jewish family that loved me and encouraged me to practice my chutzpah. That meant cheering me on in all my endeavors, building my self esteem, bolstering my confidence and celebrating my curiosity and out-going personality.

My mother and father doted on me and my little sister Bedonna. Both of us were treasured among our extended Jewish family, with aunts and uncles, grandparents, cousins, and "honorary" family members all weighing in on any important decision we were going to make. There was plenty of protocol laid out by the family and Mother made sure I followed it. After all, how would it look to the family if I didn't measure up?

All my childhood I was surrounded by people who used chutzpah. This is a very misunderstood word in the American dictionaries. It is a Jewish word that describes having a lot of nerve to go after whatever you want. It's asking for favors, requesting upgrades, negotiating prices and trying to get the best out of whatever the situation. Growing up, my examples of chutzpah were never underhanded or of questionable morals. I don't remember anyone in my family trying to cheat someone; they just practiced solid, common sense negotiating. My role-models were advocates, pro-active and clever, always looking out for the best for the family.

I was encouraged early in life about my chutzpah by my family, often overhearing comments between my aunts like, "Ahhhh! She's got chutzpah." I don't know if you can actually learn chutzpah; I think it's a kind of courage or advocacy born into your personality. And I was blessed with it!

I don't really think about using chutzpah — it just comes naturally. And one of my favorite ways is in negotiating transactions. I'm never mean or demanding; I try to be sensitive to how it's being received. Usually, everyone is just having fun with me and my negotiations. It never hurts to ask, and people are often very receptive to my requests.

It usually happens something like this: First I go after the goal. I tell the seller what I want, and what I'm willing to pay. Then I listen to the answer; then counter offer. I recognize the challenge and focus on how to tackle it. Then I keep talking and before long, people just agree with me.

Recently my husband, Clyde and I decided to buy a new car. Clyde let me do all the negotiation over the price of the new car and we drove away in a beautiful new car well under the sticker price. To me, practicing chutzpah is simply "the art of asking for favors." And as much as I like to ask for favors, I try to pay them back whenever I can. For example, you can be sure that I will refer all my friends to that salesman that sold us our new car.

Years ago, my friend Lynn and I went to Sears, just on a casual shopping trip. I had been looking for a new mirror to replace the one that hung over my dresser, and wandering in the furniture section I found one that was on a half price sale for $175. I looked it over carefully, and decided that I didn't really need a new mirror, but this one might work; if the price was right. I felt the sparkle of chutzpah awaken my senses and approached the salesman.

"I'm kind of interested in that mirror," I told him. "But I'm not in a position to pay $175. How about half?"

The salesman looked at me and pushed up his glasses. "Okay," he replied and he reached for his sales receipt book.

Hmmm... I started to wonder if he would go lower. The mirror didn't match anything else in the store. I started to look it over closer to see if there were any flaws.

"Okay," the young man said. "That's $87.50, plus tax." He started to tear the receipt from his pad.

"Oh, that's still a lot of money," I said, "And I really don't need that mirror. I was just browsing."

"Well, how much do you think it's worth?" my salesman asked, pulling his pen back out of his pocket.

I ran my hand over the frame of the mirror, noting a tiny scratch on the back side. "Oh, I don't know. Maybe $50. But...."

"I don't think so. That's a lot less than the price," the young man said, adjusting his glasses and straightening his name plate. I noticed it said "John" on it. "I'd have to ask my manager."

"Okay John," I said. "Can you ask him? I can't pay $87 for a mirror, but maybe if the price was just a bit cheaper I could."

Lynn was wandering around the furniture, looking at sofas,

and she came back to see if I was going to buy the mirror. Just as she walked up John returned and said, "Okay, my manager agreed that since we don't have any of the matching pieces, we can let you have it for $50."

"Well, that's still a lot for a scratched mirror," I told him. "It has a scratch on it back here. See? And I don't really need it." Lynn was watching in fascination.

John raised his eyebrows and pushed his glasses back up. "So what do you think it's worth?" He was grinning at me, enjoying the barter. "How low would we have to go to make the sale?"

"Well, I don't know, maybe $25," I said, smiling at him.

"I'll go check," John said, with a chuckle. "I know we have a big shipment of furniture coming Monday, and we need the room." He left with a spring in his step and returned a few minutes later.

"Okay, the manager said I can sell it for $25 to you, if you take it home today," John reached for his receipt book once again.

"Oh, I don't know, I really don't need it," I said hesitating. "Maybe if it was like, well... maybe $10 I could afford it. But now that I think about it, it's not really that important to me."

John put his receipt pad back into his jacket pocket and looked at me. "Ten dollars?" he asked. "Ten dollars is what you'll pay for the mirror? You're not serious."

"Well, maybe," I said. "Could you at least go and ask for me?"

"Sure," John said, shaking his head slowly, "Why not?" He exited the showroom floor one more time for the manager's office. I noticed he walked with a little less bounce in his step.

By now Lynn had lost interest in looking at sofas and she was at my side, speechless, wondering what was about to happen. We waited patiently to see what John could find out for me about lowering the price of the mirror.

This time John returned with the manager, a balding middle-aged man, who introduced himself and asked me about my interest in the mirror.

"Hello there," the manager said extending his hand in greeting. "I see you're interested in this mirror."

I shook his hand and said, "Yes, thank you. John has been so helpful with all my questions. I appreciate how kind he's been."

"Well, that's good to hear," the manager said. "So how can I help you?"

"Well, you see, I don't have to have a mirror," I told him. "But this one might work if the price was right." I waited, casually. I remembered John's comment that there was a big shipment of furniture due to arrive and that they needed to clear the showroom. John and I had laughed so much throughout this negotiation that I felt like he was my friend.

The manager shifted his weight and crossed his arms. "Well, what do you think is an affordable price?" he asked.

"I just don't know," I said. "I mean, it might work, in my bedroom, but I really don't need it. I just don't know..."

"Well, you and John have been talking about this mirror for awhile now," the manager said. "What is your bottom line offer?"

I looked the mirror over carefully one last time, running my hand all around the frame and checking the back for any damage. Finally I turned to the manager and said, "Well, I guess if you really want to get rid of it, I could take it off your hands for $3."

Lynn and John were both standing behind the manager. Lynn's eye's opened wide and her mouth dropped open in surprise. John was shaking his head silently and grinning from ear to ear in disbelief.

The manager looked at me and then at the salesman John, "Three dollars? Three dollars! You want me to sell you a $300 mirror for $3?" he demanded incredulously.

"Well, it's up to you, sir," I said. "I'm sorry I took up so much of your time." I started to turn to leave the showroom.

The manager let out a long sigh, then looked at John. "Write it up," he said to the young salesman, and then he turned on his heel and walked back to his office.

John chuckled as he wrote the receipt for the mirror and then took me to the cash register where I paid the $3 plus tax, for the mirror. The kind young salesman wrapped the mirror up in brown paper for me as I waited.

"Thank you, John," I said as I gathered my purse and bent to lift the mirror. "You have been so helpful. I'm going to tell all my friends to shop here and ask for you."

It was then when I realized that the mirror was far too heavy for me to carry. I tried to pick it up, but it just barely rocked a bit on the counter. John was watching me.

"John," I said fearfully, "I can't lift it."

John burst into laughter. "I'll carry it to the car for you," he said hoisting the mirror over his shoulder. He walked out to the parking lot with Lynn and me, and carefully placed the mirror in the backseat of my car.

When I started the car Lynn burst into hysterical laughter. "I can't believe what I just witnessed," Lynn said, wiping her eyes. "I can't wait to try that for myself!"

The next Saturday Lynn tried the same approach when she went to buy a new desk. But it didn't work. She didn't have the gift of chutzpah.

I have learned in my walk with God, to use chutzpah in my prayer life. I have come to realize that God wants me to talk to Him and ask for his help in everything. It's not negotiating with

God, it's simply praying, smiling and waiting as I sit back to watch how He unfolds His answers in my life. In the next chapter, you'll see how I never hesitate to go before God and pray with chutzpah.

SNAPSHOT 2

Praying for Palms

I talk to God on a regular basis. I usually start my morning with a Bible reading and a devotion and prayer. I also talk to God throughout my day, asking Him not only for the big things in life but also for the little things. And He answers! Some people don't think you should bother God with unimportant things, but I disagree. I think God likes to hear from us, and I enjoy asking God for help and watching how He answers. I am excited to see how God answers prayer, and over the years I've learned that God just might answer my prayers anywhere. It makes me think of a decorating problem I had awhile ago.

My daughter Lori and her husband Mark were pastoring a new church plant about 15 miles from my home. They were planning a big event at their church with a Hawaiian theme. Mark asked me to be in charge of the decorations. I love that sort of thing and pride myself in being creative. Mark gave me a very small budget to decorate a room for 300 people with a luau theme, and I went to work.

The budget wasn't small – it was very small. But I love a challenge, and the wheels in my head were spinning as I planned how to turn this plain gymnasium into a tropical paradise with practically no money. I began, just like I do with all of my projects, by asking God to give me ideas, materials and inspiration, and before long, I had Hawaiian centerpieces made of coconuts, pineapple and tropical flowers. Everything I needed just sort of fell into place, except that I needed palm leaves to use as the base for all the decorations. Palm leaves would anchor the theme across the room, give a continuity of color and definitely set the tropical theme.

"Lord, I need palm leaves," I prayed. I asked Lori to send out a message to all our team members to scour their neighborhoods for palm trees that needed pruning. I checked the florist shops and nurseries, but palm leaves were far beyond my meager budget, so I continued to hope and pray that someone would find some palm leaves for our luau.

Lori sent out another message to our team. "Please pray for palm leaves." She wrote. "They are far too expensive for us to buy, so please pray for palm leaves." But no palm leaves turned up.

I looked outside at our Northern California landscape. There were a few palms here and there, but it was nothing like Florida or Southern California, where palm branches grow everywhere. Since every detail of the decorating plan had fallen into place by faith, I felt confident that God would provide us with palm leaves, but the day before the event, I still hadn't found any. I felt bad that I had let Mark down; the decorations would be okay, but nothing as spectacular as I had planned if we had had palm branches.

Our family meets for breakfast every Saturday morning at a local McDonalds restaurant. As Clyde and I arrived at the restaurant that Saturday morning, I felt resigned that we would have the luau tomorrow without the palm leaves. "Lord, can you show me a different way?" I asked before we met Mark and Lori inside.

We met Mark and Lori, our son Tim and his wife Michelle and a handful of grandchildren in a corner booth. Lori took one look at me and grabbed her phone to check her messages to see if anyone had found palm branches. She shook her head silently. No one had palm leaves.

We all ordered our coffee, smoothies, egg McMuffins and hash browns and sat around the table chatting, laughing, and just catching up on the family gossip when Michelle looked out the window behind me and began to shriek. She couldn't say anything; she waved her hands up and down and screamed. Finally she just pointed.

Out in front of McDonalds, a pickup truck was parked, overflowing with palm branches. There were so many palm branches in the pickup bed, you couldn't even see out of the back window of the cab.

I jumped up and ran out to the parking lot, but no one was out there. I ran back in to the restaurant and started asking different diners, "Is that your pickup? Is that your truck out there with the palm leaves?"

No one would answer me. They all acted like I was crazy. In fact, they were afraid of me. I was so excited rushing from one table to another, asking who owned the truck with the palms. I couldn't get anyone to admit that they were driving the truck with the palm leaves God had just delivered. I was frantic with worry that someone might drive off with them before I could explain that I wanted them.

Finally, I found the manager of McDonalds, who spoke Spanish. I told her that I wanted to know if I could have the palm branches and she located the right patrons for me. She acted as my interpreter, explained the whole story in Spanish and once the men understood, they were more than willing to let me have those branches. In gratitude, Mark bought breakfast for the three landscapers.

Mark had driven his Jeep to McDonalds that day and he had a pocket knife. He put the back seat of the Jeep down, and

Mark started carefully cutting the palm leaves with his knife and then stacked them neatly in the Jeep. Lori, Michelle and I were screaming and celebrating around the truck at how wonderfully God had provided.

As silly as it may seem, I believe God cared if I had palm leaves for my event. I know that God was smiling on me that morning in McDonalds. He was delivering those palm leaves to me as only God could do it. We tried on our own to get palm leaves, and it didn't work. But when I asked God, He did it for me. I didn't doubt that God could provide palm leaves for a church luau. I just didn't expect it to be at McDonalds with a whole landscape truck full of palm branches.

Clyde often prays that our faith will grow "another notch," each day. That morning, at McDonald's, all of us felt our faith grow several notches as Mark loaded all those palm leaves into his Jeep. And I think perhaps the owner of the truck who brought the palm leaves was celebrating that morning, too. Not only did he get a free breakfast and a free unloading of the branches destined for the dump, he also had a great story to tell his friends about the women who were screaming with excitement and dancing around the truck in the McDonald's parking lot.

SNAPSHOT 3

Growing Up Jewish

My earliest memories are laced with the love and affection of a large extended Jewish family, in and out of our lives each day, while the drama of World War II hovered over us. Our lives were wrapped in a family-related social world that focused on our Jewish culture and pride. Mother often told me, "Be proud that you are Jewish!" And I was.

Mother was the epitome of the stereotypical Jewish mother —overprotective, critical and controlling, always molding me into a better version of me. If anyone had ever suggested that any of these traits were inappropriate, Mother would have simply asked, "Why?"

Daddy was a very traditional Jewish father. He was a successful businessman, as well as a devoted family man, who worked hard to provide a stable home and lifestyle for us. He was often quiet, introspective and thoughtful while Mother was vivacious, spoke her mind and always talked with her hands waving in the air. Mother and Daddy were a united team in parenting and disciplining me and my sister Bedonna, most of the time.

Mother had high standards for just about everything, and she insisted that I follow them. Every day Mother would get all dressed up, put on her high heels and take the bus downtown to meet her sisters for lunch. She required that I always be dressed up as well. I learned to love fashion early in life and enjoyed coordinating outfits, accessorizing and looking my best. I loved to wear stylish clothes, but I was never allowed to wear slacks, because after all, "What would people think?"

Mother taught me that being a Jewish mother gave her special rights and privileges to meddle. She had opinions about everything that concerned me, and so did all of my aunts and grandmother. It was common for the whole family to weigh in with an opinion about all sorts of decisions about me, just as they did with each other. If I wanted a new haircut or a to go to summer camp, my aunts and grandmother would all share their opinions, often arguing with each other while I watched and listened. It was fascinating sometimes to hear their comments, wondering if I would be persuaded to one of their opinions before the discussion was over. It never occurred to me that they shouldn't be involved; they were always involved. Whenever there was a family gathering, there was always a cacophony of chatter. They all talked at once, and if someone had a point to make, rather than wait for a break in the conversation, he or she would just speak up louder. Somehow we all understood what the other was saying.

Mother was proud to show Bedonna and me off to the family. She took us to Gilmore's Tea Room where we practiced our best table manners in our fancy dresses. Many Friday nights we would get dressed up in our finest clothes to go to the synagogue. When services were over, there was always food and festivities and Friday nights were always filled with much joy and kibitzing. We learned to celebrate the High Holy Days – Yom Kippur, the Day of Atonement and Rosh Hashanah, the beginning of Jewish New Year.

My cousin, Larry, was my best friend when I was a child. He and I played at Lake Michigan in the summer or just sat on our front porch talking and talking as we watched the fireflies glow in the dark. Larry and I didn't have to have an agenda of things to do to have fun. We just enjoyed being together and when we'd get home, we would call each other and continue to chat. Mother always thought of Larry as the son she didn't have. As children Larry and I felt so safe and loved in our little Jewish community and neither of us thought our lives were different from the rest of the world. We were surrounded by Jewish people, customs, traditions and beliefs and seldom did our family socialize outside of the Jewish community.

In the summer, each Sunday the entire extended family went to South Haven Beach for a day of swimming, sunbathing and a huge family picnic that always included smoked fish. Weddings were always a joyous occasion. The gowns were so beautiful and the parties and receptions associated with weddings often include elaborate feasts, great music and dancing. Like most little girls, I talked about the day Daddy would walk me down the aisle at the synagogue, and I dreamed of a fancy white lace wedding gown with a sparkly tiara. Mother always agreed, reminding me to be on the lookout for a nice Jewish boy who would measure up to the family standards.

I was keenly aware that the extended family was watching me throughout my childhood. When I was about 16, I was in a play. The whole family went to see it. In the first act, I walked out onto the stage, just about to say my line and my Aunt Clara shouted, "Oy Vey!" She was so proud to see me on stage and wanted everyone around her to know it.

Unlike many of my Jewish girlfriends, I didn't have a Bat Mitzvah; instead, my friend Sandy and I were confirmed. That suited me just fine because a confirmation didn't require me to learn all the Hebrew passages. Mother and Daddy gave me a beautiful new outfit to wear for my confirmation and threw a huge party in my honor where all the family gave me money. There was a ceremony, followed by dancing and a traditional Jewish feast. It remains a wonderful memory, not because it marked anything special in my faith, but because it felt so good to see the family proud of me. The family thought of my confirmation as a spiritual experience, but I was caught up in the fun of festivities, gifts, new clothes and counting my money; successfully fulfilling my duty as a Jewish daughter.

SNAPSHOT 4

Jewish Daughter, Christian Wife

I was about 18 when my best girlfriend, Arlene, coerced me into a blind date. She had a new boyfriend named Clyde, and he had a friend in town. Arlene wanted me to go out with the friend. I hadn't met Arlene's new beau, but she was crazy about him. So as a favor to Arlene, I agreed to go on a double date with them, even though I rarely dated Gentile boys. Arlene and I got all dressed up for our dinner and dancing date. I accessorized my high fashion outfit right down to the rhinestone cigarette holder I loved to carry.

My date was a great dancer, very good looking and a smooth talker. We had a pretty good time, but I was distracted because I was observing Arlene and Clyde, and I couldn't figure out what she saw in him. He was tall and ruggedly attractive in a John Wayne sort of way, but he was so rude! When he was passing around snacks to everyone, he went right by me. And even worse — he seemed to enjoy embarrassing me by skipping me. Why would he do that?

Arlene and Clyde, my blind date and I became a foursome and went out a few more times, but before long, I knew that the relationship was not going anywhere. During that time Clyde lowered his guard and became cordial to me, and that's when I became aware of what a nice guy Clyde was. Now I could see why Arlene cared for him.

Arlene was Catholic and Clyde was Protestant, and Clyde and I started meeting casually to discuss their differences in religion. I counseled Clyde over Cokes, wondering in the back of my mind what he would think about me being Jewish. I was torn on meeting with Clyde to help him plan a future with Arlene, when I was beginning to think Clyde might be an okay guy for me. But I cared for Arlene so much; she was my best friend. The truth was though that I cared more for myself. Each time Clyde and I met, it was under the pretense of talking about the relationship between Clyde and Arlene. But we were really developing our own relationship.

I kept asking myself, "How could I possibly hurt Arlene in this way?" But I did. Eventually we went to Arlene and told her the truth. She was crushed.

Clyde and Arlene broke up and he began formally courting me without my parents' knowledge. They would never have approved of Clyde, simply because he wasn't Jewish. So Clyde would meet me after work, and I would lie to my parents about my dates. Before long, I was head over heels in love with this strong, handsome guy who would pick me up and take me to another town for pizza or swimming at Gun Lake with other couples.

I told Clyde right from the beginning that there was no way I could get serious about a relationship with him because my parents would never approve of him. Clyde listened, assured me that he understood my fears, then he'd start kissing me, and I'd forget all about it. We didn't plan on falling in love or getting married. We just enjoyed the stolen moments. We would drive up to the lake and listen to Doris Day on the radio. The song "Three Coins in the Fountain," was popular then, along with the song "Young Love." It was so romantic to be with my handsome forbidden boyfriend.

I finally conceded that I was in love with Clyde and confessed to my parents that I had developed a strong attraction to Clyde. Their reaction was exactly what I expected to hear regarding any prospective son-in-law who had the misfortune to be born Gentile. First there were huge arguments which included a lot of screaming and threats, and eventually my parents began sending me to Chicago each weekend to visit my grandparents. In Chicago, they thought I would be protected from that evil Gentile boy and that I could be distracted with proper Jewish friends. I was required to attend a variety of parties and events, peppered with plenty of Jewish men to turn my heart from Clyde.

But Clyde and I had fallen deeply in love, and love does find a way. Clyde's family lived in Chicago, so he would drive his 1953 Ford to Chicago along the rail road tracks when my train pulled out. I would sit in a window seat on the train and blow kisses to Clyde as he drove beside the train. When I arrived at the train station in Chicago, Clyde picked me up and then pretended to be my taxi driver to and from my grandmother's house and the train station. He stayed overnight with his sister, who lived in a suburb, just a short drive from my grandmother's house. It was an elaborate plan, but it worked, and I looked forward to those secret moments to and from the train station and to my grandmother's house each week.

Each Saturday night I would be sent on a pre-arranged "date" with a nice Jewish boy who took me to a night club for a fancy evening of dinner and dancing. All the while I was counting the hours until my "taxi driver" would arrive at my grandmother's house to take me to the bus station on Sunday. The men I went out with were fine, respectable, successful young men, all Jewish and all proper prospects for a husband.

But the dates were so boring, except for one night when the night club was held up at gunpoint!

A robber came into the club, waving a gun around and demanding money. "Get under the tables!" the cry went out, so in my silky white dress, high heels and teased hair I climbed under the table for about a half hour, anticipating the gunfire and bloodbath that I'd seen in the movies. My date put his arm around me to protect me, but I felt repulsed rather than grateful. This date was nothing more than a duty in kindness to my parents. Even though this handsome young man was in his last year at MIT and considered a very good catch by all my aunts and grandmother, I was not interested. I had already given my heart to Clyde.

At first the robbery didn't even seem real. "Jeepers!" I told my date, "I've never been on a date under a table before." But when people started screaming and the robber began demanding money, it wasn't funny anymore. That's when I was angry at the irony of the situation. I thought, "So Mother and Daddy sent me here to protect me, and now I'm going to be shot!"

Finally the music started playing again, and the police arrived to tell us we could get up from under the table. My date helped me up, and I ran to the phone in the ladies' room to call Clyde. He comforted me on the phone for awhile and then I returned back to the table and then home with my date.

I wanted to please my parents, but I wanted to live my life with Clyde. We kept up the charade of me going to Chicago each weekend, with Clyde being my taxi driver to and from the train station, until one Sunday on my return trip. Clyde and I decided I would skip the train and simply ride home with him. Back in the fifties, cars didn't have bucket seats or gear shifts on the floor. I could practically sit on Clyde's lap for the entire 150 mile trip. Things were going splendidly, driving down the green-hilled country roads, until large storm clouds loomed on the horizon and marble-sized hail began to pelt our car. Clyde slowed down, but before long, the road was impassable and he had to pull over as we watched black clouds spit jagged lightning bolts and felt loud booming thunder shake the ground. I didn't know what would be worse, not getting to the train station on time to meet my parents or dying in the storm.

When I didn't get off the train, my parents were alarmed and immediately called my grandparents to find out if I was ill, or why I had remained in Chicago. They were sure I had missed the train.

My grandmother's response was calm and unworried. "Sadie, I don't know who that taxi driver is, but she's in love with him." This launched a whole new level of my parents' futile fight to end my love for Clyde.

I have never been so unhappy as when I tried to stop loving Clyde. We quit seeing each other to honor Mother and Daddy's request, and my heart was broken. One day I just couldn't stand it anymore, and I decided to drive out on Highway 37 to Clyde's sister's house about 30 miles away. I thought maybe she would have some sympathy or wisdom to share with me. Along the way I recognized a green Ford coming from the other direction, and I slowed down. It was Clyde. We both pulled over on opposite sides of the road and ran to embrace in the middle of the highway. Right there, with cars flying by us and honking for us to get out of the road, we made a vow to forge a life together.

We knew that the first thing we had to do was resolve our religious differences. Clyde agreed to talk to a Rabbi, and I agreed to meet with a minister. The appointments worked out that my meeting with the Christian pastor was first.

I was surprised when, instead of going to a church, Clyde drove me to a small, modest home in a city outside of Kalamazoo. The pastor offered us a seat in the living room. He began by asking me questions about my family and growing up Jewish. He then asked if he could explain some things to me from the Bible.

I agreed. I had looked at a Bible before, but never actually read one. I had gone to synagogue nearly every Friday night of my life, but I didn't really know much about the religious part of being Jewish. I knew how to pray to God for help, and I knew that Jews believed in one God and none other. Aside from that, my Jewish heritage was more about culture and the fellowship of Friday nights.

The pastor started in the Old Testament, and I found the information he shared fascinating and interesting. I recognized some of the verses that he'd said because I'd heard them on Friday nights at the synagogue. I relaxed a bit, and the pastor asked me if I had ever looked at the New Testament.

The pastor began to explain to me that Jesus was the promised Messiah of the Jewish faith. I didn't know what the Messiah was. All those years of synagogue had consisted of traditional prayers with little instruction. There were no sermons or lessons. I never paid attention until the service was over, and it was time for the party to begin. Being Jewish to me had little to do with worship or God; it was about the holidays that we celebrated and the enormous, rich culture that engulfed us.

When the pastor began to talk about Jesus, it made me nervous. I'd been taught that we did not believe in Jesus – and that there is only one God. But when the minister went on to tell me that Jesus and God were the one true God, and that belief in Jesus offered peace, heaven and forgiveness of sin, it hit home with me. I knew that I had sinned. I felt guilty about all the lies I had been telling to be with Clyde and especially for the pain I was causing my parents. I was going against everything that they held dear to their hearts. But Clyde was to as dear to me, as tradition was to them.

The pastor's information that day offered peace and that sounded so good to me. I had such a vacant feeling inside me all the time. I was always searching through friends, parties, clothes, for something to make me feel satisfied, safe and secure. My security came from traveling, events, clothes, parties, where I would feel content for awhile, but as soon as it was over, I would have to re-start the process. I felt as if I drifted from one social engagement or fashion trend to another.

But this kind minister told me there was a purpose to my life. I wanted to know what mine was. "Gerrie, may I read something to you from the New Testament?" he asked.

I nodded nervously. And then he opened up his Bible to John 3:16 in the New Testament. "For God so loved the world, that He gave his only son. That whoever believes in Him shall not perish but have eternal life."

"Gerrie," he said. "There is more to life than just having friends, going places and dressing up." That resonated within me. He had described exactly what my life was. How did he know this? He didn't even know me! Even though I knew what he said was true, I was shaking inside.

As he talked more about what it meant to be a believer and to have a relationship with God, somehow I just knew that what he was saying was true even though I'd never heard these things before. Jesus was God. What he was saying made sense and was probably true. He seemed to be a man who represented God, and I trusted him. He wasn't trying to talk me into anything; he was just explaining what being a believer meant. Finally he asked me if I would like to receive Jesus into my life. I knew I couldn't, so I politely declined. I thanked him, and he walked Clyde and me out to the car. As Clyde opened the car door for me, I began crying.

"What's wrong?" Clyde asked.

I didn't know what was wrong. I didn't understand that the Holy Spirit was working in my life at that point.

I looked at the minister and said. "I don't even know myself what's wrong." In my heart I was afraid to leave this man of God because he told me I could have happiness, peace and forgiveness, all things that I craved. And, yet, I was walking away.

The pastor looked at me kindly. "Gerrie," he said, "You are at a crossroad in your life, and it's up to you to make a decision. You can invite God into your life, but it has to be your decision, not something you do to please Clyde or me."

"I do," I sobbed. "I do want God in my life."

And so we went back into the house and, with child-like faith, I invited Jesus into my heart to forgive me where I failed, and to be my God.

I felt the happiest I had ever been in my life. And as Jesus entered my life, I experienced unspeakable joy. Mixed with that joy was the biggest relief I had ever known. First I was crying because I was frightened, then I was crying because I was so happy that I had done it. In the back of my mind I was also thinking that it was too bad that I would never be able to tell my parents about this moment.

When we drove away that afternoon, Clyde and I were talking about his family and my family, and how both of them had insisted that marriages could not be of two different faiths. Well that wasn't a problem anymore, so we decided that since we were so crazy in love we would elope. I didn't stop to think about what an important weekend it was at my house. My sister Bedonna was being confirmed the very next day. The entire family was busy preparing for her party and celebration. I was young and foolish and wrapped up in myself and this handsome young man.

I ran to the store to purchase a new pink outfit for the wedding. Clyde and I picked up two of our friends to be our witnesses and we dropped by Clyde's parents' house to tell them what our plans were. Then we sped away to Angola, Indiana to elope.

SNAPSHOT 5

Early Married Years

As I said, "I do," I thought to myself, "I did what?" I was trembling in fear, as I sent a telegram from Angola to my parents; and then the craziness really began. I was a young Jewish daughter, the darling of the family, newly married to a Gentile. My parents, aunts, uncles, and grandparents were all outraged. I had dishonored my parents and my culture. Bedonna's confirmation had been ruined by the outrage of my family over what I had done.

Clyde and I returned to our hometown to a little apartment and began our married life. Clyde had grown up in a Christian home, but he was just going through the motions of living a Christian life. I was so new in the faith, that I didn't know how to live for the Lord. It didn't take long for the honeymoon to be over and reality to set in.

Adjusting to married life was a huge challenge, and it was increased by the judgment of my family. They wanted me to leave Clyde and my new religion and come back to my Jewish roots. Clyde and I seemed to fight about everything and as the actuality of marriage set in, I was fearful that my parents might be right. Especially, because prior to our marriage, I was oblivious to the fact that Clyde had a drinking problem. During our courtship, Clyde didn't drink until he dropped me off after our dates, and then he then went out with the guys. I didn't know how to deal with this man that I loved who elected to spend time drinking on his way home from work and gambling away his paycheck.

The first five years we had a roller coaster marriage. Our lives were filled with parties, and I spent money as fast as Clyde could make it. I resented the money Clyde spent on drinking, so I spent money on myself, the children and our home. As we began to fill our home with children, I could see that this lifestyle was not the kind of environment that I had dreamed of. It wasn't the lifestyle Clyde's mother had hoped for either. One day we received a letter from her inviting us to watch Dr. Billy Graham's television series for the next four Saturday nights. Out of respect for Clyde's mother, we watched the series and were inspired by Dr. Graham's lectures, so Clyde and I decided together that in about 20 years, we would both make changes in our lives reflective of Dr. Graham's invitation. But what we didn't know was that God was moving in our hearts, bit by bit, nurturing tiny seeds of faith that had the potential to bloom into deep-rooted Christian commitment.

Clyde and I continued to squabble over everything, and Clyde began drinking heavily. There was an unsettled edge to our relationship, and we were both terribly unhappy. One day when Clyde was driving down a road, he was so unhappy and began thinking about his childhood and how loved and happy he felt growing up. He remembered a song he used to sing as a child, and all alone in the car, Clyde began to sing, "Oh, how I love Jesus. Oh, how I love Jesus. Oh how I love Jesus, because He first loved me."

Clyde still felt a sad emptiness in his heart, so he sang it again, "Oh, how I love Jesus," over and over again until he felt so convicted he stopped singing and said to himself, "Who are you kidding? You don't love Jesus." As he continued on down the road, Clyde began to think about all the ways he had disappointed God. He knew that God loved him and that Jesus was the way to heaven, but Clyde began to wonder if he was even going to make it to heaven when he died. That thought worried Clyde, and when he drove by a picnic area, he pulled over. He got out of the car and sat down at a table where he began to evaluate his life by having a talk with God. This was completely out of character for my self-confident, rugged, successful businessman husband – in fact – it was crazy! But there at that picnic table Clyde begged God to forgive him and to help him become the husband, father, son, friend and believer that God wanted him to be. Clyde felt God answer his prayer and instantly Clyde truly became a Christian in his heart and not just in words.

When Clyde came home, I knew something was different before he even walked in the house. And when he told me that he'd given his heart to the Lord that day, I was furious. What an absurd idea – he had given his heart to me! And he wasn't doing a very good job of it, either. Now I had to share his heart with God? Not only was I angry, but this new revelation frightened me.

Clyde started going to church on his own while I stayed home Sunday mornings. He even began taking the children with him on Sundays, despite the fact that I refused to help him get them ready. Eventually, my heart softened, and I accompanied Clyde to church. But I refused to go back, digging in my heels and justifying my feelings that it wasn't for me. I used every excuse I could dream up.

But one day, while I was home washing dishes, I found myself drowning in my stubbornness. I could see the startling changes in Clyde – no more drinking; no more rough language; tender attentiveness to me and the children – these were things I had wanted Clyde to change, and now I didn't even appreciate what I had. I got to my knees and asked God to forgive me for my foolish attitude and to help me make the changes in my life that I needed to fix, the same as He was doing in Clyde.

I rededicated my life to the Lord and reading my Bible took on a whole new meaning. My Bible seemed to have changed from black and white to vivid color. I began to grow spiritually, and I started looking forward to worship and prayer meetings and the fellowship of other Christians who were just as flawed as I was but also just as forgiven. Clyde's brother Wes taught me how to share my faith. In the beginning, I didn't know what I was doing. But I saw that people were thankful and responsive, and I could feel in my spirit that God was using me to tell other people about Jesus.

My approach was always casual, and I never fancied myself a "preacher." I was just so eager to share how God was working in my life that I couldn't resist sharing with my neighbors, friends or anyone who would listen. I'd usually start the conversation with "Can I tell you something God did for me today?"

They always said, "Yes," and then I'd explain how I had prayed about something specific and how God had provided exactly what I needed. I was so excited to see how God was working in my life that I couldn't wait to share it with others. I hoped that it would create a desire within others to listen to how God might be speaking to their hearts. I couldn't imagine how anyone would decline to have the same relationship with God that I had. One by one, my neighbors all began to accept the Lord, and our neighborhood began to thrive.

SNAPSHOT 6

Called To Ministry

After Clyde and I had rededicated our lives to the Lord, Clyde received a wonderful job offer, and we moved our four children to a large Victorian home in New England where Clyde became an executive for a national shoe company. Our large, sprawling backyard included a barn, something very unusual for life in the city. Clyde and I joined a church nearby, and as our faith continued to grow, we prayed about how to use that big barn for God's work. It was a large, sturdy structure that just needed a lot of cleaning to become something useful. Clyde and I decided to use the barn as a youth center for all the teens in our area.

Amazingly, all the neighbors were excited to have such a great resource in the neighborhood and supported our plan. The big barn made a great place for young people from church to gather for activities. And, after putting that idea into the Lord's hands, it seemed like the entire community wanted to get involved.

PepsiCo donated soft drink products for our barn events. That idea inspired several members of the church to build a snack bar inside. A local potato chip company donated popcorn and chips for every Friday night event. When a local restaurant closed, they donated all their dining booths for the barn. There were many horse stalls in the barn and members converted them into a bowling alley! Several ping pong tables showed up one day and those were set up in another area. Every Friday night, the barn was filled with young people who came for recreation activities as well as spiritual devotions.

My children were very young, and our youngest was just a toddler. But somehow, I found the time to plan activities, contests, speakers and events for the barn each week. Frequently, missionaries came to share their stories at the barn. Sometimes businessmen spoke to the group, always with the message of God's love and encouraging children in their faith. Soon we were filling the barn on Saturday nights too. And often the crowd would swell from the barn to our house. It didn't matter to me, because I could see many, many young people accepting the Lord into their lives.

I loved the barn and planning all the activities we held there. But I had no idea that God was using this barn to prepare me for the plan He had in store for our family. All I knew was that the more we helped people to understand the love of God and accept the love of Jesus, the more Clyde and I craved it. We had never considered going into the ministry as an occupation; this was just fun. Clyde had an excellent career and was very successful financially. But we loved serving God with our ministry in the barn.

A missionary speaker at our barn event told of how God called her to ministry. It was just before World War II when she heard God call her to travel to a specific address, but she had no money and no way to get there. She prayed for God to provide, and when she finished praying she looked down and there was a nickel on the sidewalk. It was just exactly what she needed for bus fare. As I listened to her story of faith and trusting God to provide, I wanted to have that kind of faith too.

So I prayed to have faith – strong faith – unlimited faith – and I believe that's where I began my faith walk. If God could provide a nickel on the sidewalk for her, He could provide whatever I needed too. I didn't know what our needs might be in the next few months, and I wasn't thinking of any particular needs. I just wanted that close relationship with God and the confidence that I could count on Him.

A few weeks later, I was sitting on our chocolate brown sofa that faced a big bay window, reading my Bible. The children were at school. Clyde was at his office, and the baby was napping. I was reading about the apostle Paul, who refused to use his energy for anything other than furthering the Gospel. That hit home with me because it took enormous energy to get the barn ready each week. And the barn wasn't my only responsibility. There was Sunday school, the Christian Women's Club, my four children, and a wife and a husband with whom I had an active social life in Portland; I was always on the go. This was a vivid message for me because I felt God saying, "Gerrie, I want you to serve me with all your energy." I didn't know what it all meant, but I knew it was real, and I knew that I felt differently.

That very day, before Clyde went to work in the morning, he read in the fourth chapter of Mark, verses one through seventeen, "Follow me, and I will make you fishers of men." Clyde felt God call him with that scripture, as sure as if an audible voice had boomed from the clouds. Clyde didn't mention it to me, but that morning in his office, Clyde couldn't stop thinking about it. As Clyde turned in his chair to look out over Casco Bay, he paused to take in the teal blue frothy water and the sea gulls soaring through the mist. He was supposed to be filling out work orders for the factory to make soles for shoes. As Clyde looked at the forms, he felt as if God were asking him to stop ordering soles for shoes and instead begin gathering souls for heaven.

It took Clyde until after our mid-week church service that night to tell me about his encounter earlier that day. I was stunned to realize that I had experienced my similar call from God the very same day, just hours after Clyde had. There was no denying it. God was calling us together, on the very same day, to the ministry.

But we didn't go without reservation and a lot of unanswered questions. We loved our lives in Portland. It was so much fun living near our dearest friends, Wes and Carolyn. We had enough money, the children were thriving in our big Victorian home, and we loved our church, our neighborhood – even the famous lobsters of Maine! Our lives were perfect in Portland. How could we give all of that up? And worst of all, how could I explain this divine calling to my family?

Clyde and I prayed that God would direct our new steps and provide whatever we needed to follow his plans for our ministry. The next day I went to our mailbox and found an unexpected letter from the State of Maine. It was a check, made out to Clyde for 50 cents – an overpayment on his driver's license renewal. I stood there on the porch with that check in my hand and began to tremble. It was my nickel on the sidewalk, the same as my missionary friend. Who mails a check for 50 cents? I knew that God was showing us that He would provide.

SNAPSHOT 7

The Red Negligee

One of my most treasured gifts from God is my relationship with my husband, Clyde. I pray about our marriage all the time. Back in Bible college, we wives were taught to recognize the signals of women who fall for ministers. As we learned about the role of pastors wives, we were given guidance on how to gracefully stand our ground against women on the prowl.

My husband is a tall, strikingly handsome man, and I've always had my antennae out for flirtatious women. Back in Bible college, my prayers about our marriage were laced with thanksgiving as well as asking God to strengthen and preserve us. I recall an incident long ago, when my patience was tested, but my prayers were answered.

While Clyde was attending Bible college he also worked full time. This left me at home in a small house taking care of our four children most of the time alone. We rarely saw each other, and if we did, it was never just the two of us. There was always something or someone interrupting us.

One day, Clyde ran into Hank and Rachelle, two childhood friends who had married and now lived in our region of Michigan. He brought them home to meet me and we became casual acquaintances, socializing occasionally. Clyde and I were saddened when one day we learned that Hank had suddenly passed away. Hank was a young man, and his death was untimely. We attended the memorial service for Hank and wished Rachelle the best as we left the cemetery. A few weeks later, Rachelle showed up at our house unannounced, asking Clyde to counsel her in her grief.

Clyde invited her in and did what he could to comfort Rachelle. He scheduled another appointment for the following week, squeezing it in between working full time and his full-time college load. I was sad for Rachelle, but I found myself withholding my usual Jewish hospitality with her. Clyde was so busy between working and studying and being a good father, that I thought counseling a grief-stricken friend was a lot of extra pressure. And Rachelle didn't seem to be making any progress. She continued to schedule new appointments each week, and I began to get suspicious of her motives. She had to travel a couple of hours to get to our house for counseling. It seemed to me that she could have found a qualified pastor in her town.

Rachelle arrived one night in a typical Michigan snowstorm. When it was time to go home, Rachelle was concerned that it was unsafe to travel and asked if she could spend the night. She had an overnight bag packed, waiting for her in the car. Clyde and I agreed that it probably was unsafe to travel that night so I moved the children around and prepared a room for Rachelle. I settled her in and everyone went to sleep.

The next morning, it was bitterly cold outside and the entire neighborhood was covered in snow. I rose early to make sure Clyde had breakfast before he left for school. I headed for the kitchen in my warm flannel nightgown and fuzzy slippers. I had no makeup on and my hair was mussed from sleep. I looked in the mirror and finger combed my hair. Then, just as I dashed down the staircase, I noticed grease stains on my nightgown from previous early-morning cooking splatters.

I started breakfast, and I had bacon crackling in the pan as Clyde came into the dining area and sat down at the table. I kissed him, handing him a cup of coffee and his Bible, all part of our early morning routine. As I continued with breakfast, Clyde was sipping his coffee, turning pages and writing notes, when I noticed something bright red and sparkly moving on the stairs. That's when Rachelle came floating down the stairs, into the dining area, looking like a million bucks! She was dressed in a short red negligee with a plunging neckline showing off a rather extraordinary chest, and the rest of her voluptuous body was visible through the sheer fabric. Her hair was styled, and her makeup was perfect. She looked stunning; and I was stunned.

Actually, I was shocked. It was ten below zero outside and far too cold to be wearing anything but long underwear! And, who packs a red negligee in an emergency bag for the car?! Suddenly, my intuition about Rachelle made sense. Everything I suspected that Rachelle felt for my husband was clear. She wasn't grieving; she was on the prowl for my husband in my own home!

I took one look at Clyde, and then back at Rachelle. He followed my gaze toward Rachelle and when he saw her, his eyes widened. He was surprised at first and then I could see his reaction change as Clyde realized Rachelle's intent. Clyde didn't even say, "Good morning." He just jumped up from the table, spilling his coffee and dropping his books as he exited the room quickly in embarrassment. This left me in the room with Rachelle alone. A Jewish woman is rarely speechless, but my jaw dropped, and there was nothing coming out of my mouth. I just stood there noting the stark contrast between us, me in my stained flannel night gown and she in her sexy red negligee.

My first thought was that I wanted her out of my house. I'd heard about women like this, but I never expected one to show up for breakfast. I had four children who at any moment were going to arrive in my dining room. There were bound to be some questions when they saw Rachelle's outfit and their father absent.

There was a long, pregnant silence between Rachelle and me. I handed her a cup and began to pour coffee into it. I looked into her eyes, and I wished I had the courage to ask her why she was dressed in this skimpy nightgown when it was ten degrees below zero outside. But instead I just asked her how she liked her eggs. I started scrambling eggs, cracking them hard and whipping them with far more fury than ever before until the children came downstairs looking for breakfast and the room filled with our regular morning chatter.

Rachelle wandered upstairs, got dressed and left our house just as the children were finishing their breakfasts. By this time, I was angry at her brazen attempt to invade my marriage. After the children left for school, I packed up our youngest son and went to see Mr. Miles, my mentor and confidant at the Bible college. I was a peace-loving woman, but I was so upset. I was ready for war!

"I cannot believe she came strutting into my own kitchen dressed like that!" I said to Mr. Miles in my fury.

Mr. Miles smiled warmly and patted my hand. He was very sympathetic and let me vent my rage until he asked me, "So what do you want from this, Gerrie?"

"I want her out of my house and away from my husband!" I said through my tears.

"Okay," Mr. Miles said. "Try this. The next time she calls to schedule a grief counseling appointment with Clyde, schedule it for a time when you know Clyde won't be home."

I liked the sound of this idea.

Mr. Miles continued, "Then, when she arrives, you answer the door, explain sweetly that Clyde is far too busy studying, going to college full time and working full time, so you will be assuming the role of grief counselor."

Sure enough, Rachelle called a few days later to book another appointment with Clyde. I followed Mr. Miles' advice, and it worked perfectly. When Rachelle came to the door, and I explained that I would be her new grief counselor, she quickly made an excuse to leave immediately, and we never heard from her again.

To celebrate, I threw out that stained flannel nightgown!

SNAPSHOT 8

A Big Surprise

Clyde and I have a lot of fun in our marriage. There is a great deal of joy in the Mills' household, and I love to make Clyde laugh. For years I have asked God to help me keep the fun in our relationship. I never ever want either Clyde or I to take our marriage for granted, so I have often asked God to help me find creative ways to keep the spark going in our married life.

Early in Clyde's pastoral career, he was the pastor at a rural country church in Quincy, Michigan. Our home in Quincy was located five miles from town, right next door to the church. It was far from traffic and we had virtually no neighbors within shouting distance. It was a tranquil setting amid rolling fertile farmland, large leafy trees and scattered wildlife. Our living room faced the country road that led to our house and had a huge floor to ceiling picture window overlooking our beautiful country setting.

Each day my role was to fix breakfast for everyone, and get the children off to school very early to catch the school bus. Clyde's daily routine included driving into town for coffee right after the children boarded the bus. From the first day of our marriage, I wanted to keep the spice in our relationship, and so I was always eager to find ways to show Clyde how much I adored him. I liked to put little love notes in his pockets or sneak up behind him to give him a hug when he least expected it. I liked color and sparkle in my wardrobe and it just seemed to spill into my marriage as well. In my morning devotions, I often asked God to inspire me with creative ways to keep the romance in our marriage.

One morning, as the children boarded the school bus, and I was cleaning up the breakfast dishes, I had a great idea to make Clyde smile and spark up his day. Standing there in the kitchen dressed in my blue and lavender flowered nightgown and robe, I scrubbed the frying pan and giggled as I waited in anticipation. Just as usual, Clyde came into the kitchen, picked up his car keys from the peg by the door and kissed me goodbye as he headed for coffee.

As soon as the door closed, I went to the big picture window in the living room and drew the drapes open wide. I took off my robe and waited, looking down the road each way to see if there were any cars on the road. It was just 7 a.m., and there wasn't a soul on the road.

It seemed like it took forever for Clyde to get the car going, and I couldn't see him or the car from the window. Then, finally I caught site of our car rolling down our long driveway, then it turned onto the road, about 50 feet from where I was standing. As soon as the car was in line with the window, I threw my nightgown up over my head, giving Clyde a full view of me standing in the window totally nude.

"This will make him smile," I thought to myself smugly.

I laughed and pulled the nightgown back down, waiting to see if the car stopped, ran into the ditch or backed up, when I noticed not one, but two heads in the car!

I fell to the floor in disbelief. Where did that second person come from? Who in the world could be with Clyde at 7 a.m.? Nobody had knocked on the door. Nobody had called, and no one had been at our house. It was too far for me to see Clyde's facial reaction to my prank, but I could see his head leaning forward over the steering wheel, so I knew that he had seen me... and so had the other person in the car!

It was my most embarrassing moment.

When I looked outside later that morning, I was mortified to find an Indiana State patrol car parked in our driveway. Later I learned that an Indiana State Trooper had wanted to talk to Clyde that morning. The man knew Clyde's routine, so he was waiting for Clyde as he exited our house and simply climbed into our car when Clyde left for coffee.

It had never occurred to me that Clyde might not be alone in the car that morning. The children were off to school. We had no neighbors within walking distance, and I was certain that I was alone and that Clyde would be driving along that road by himself. When I realized that it was a policeman in the car, I thought I might die from humiliation or worse – be arrested for indecent exposure.

Clyde took it all in stride and assured me that the state trooper was looking the other way when they drove by our big window with the surprise floorshow. I will probably never know for sure, but there is some satisfaction in knowing that while that big surprise happened over 30 years ago, it still makes Clyde smile.

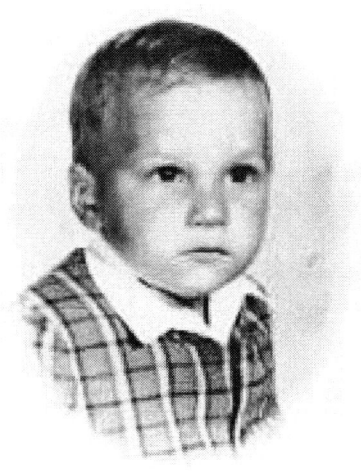

SNAPSHOT 9

Lost or Left Behind

While Clyde was in Bible college he also worked a full time job. My time was spent taking care of our children and running our household. I was determined not to complain to Clyde about anything because I wanted him to be able to focus entirely on his studies. I took it upon myself to manage the kids and house by myself as much as possible.

Caring for four small children alone is a daunting task. I was also serving in ministry at our church with plenty of responsibilities there each Sunday. Getting four children dressed for church, bundled up and in the car, all on a strict schedule, was often a comedy of errors. I was blessed to always have Clyde available if I needed him during those hectic years, but my experience trying to be both mother and father while Clyde studied gave me a tender heart for the single parent.

I remember one Sunday morning, when we were all ready to go, I realized that Lori was missing a shoe. I hunted everywhere I could think of – under the bed, in the hamper and under the couch, but I could not find that shoe. I had polished the shoes on Saturday, and somehow between the polishing and Sunday morning, one little white shoe disappeared. Mike and Andy pitched in to help look and before long the boys had the bedding torn off all the beds and the cushions on the couch were askew and yet Lori's shoe was still lost.

Clyde helped the boys tie their ties, while I clipped a little red bow in Lori's hair.

"I can't imagine where that shoe is," I told Clyde. "We have looked everywhere!"

"Well, it has to be here," Clyde said matter-of-factly. "You just haven't looked in the right place yet." I looked around at the whole house practically tipped upside down and wondered where the right place could possibly be.

Clyde joined the search, looking in the same places I had, but he couldn't find it either – we were still missing one little white shoe. Finally Clyde said, "We have to leave now, or we'll be late for church."

Lori and I exclaimed together, "We can't go to church with only one shoe!"

"Well, if we can't find it, you'll have to," Clyde answered.

"Give me five more minutes," I told Clyde. "Let me look again in Lori's room."

Five minutes later, I still couldn't find that little white shoe. Tears were welling in Lori's eyes as I helped her into her little red coat. Clyde picked Lori up and carried her to the car as she sobbed. The boys giggled all the way to church trying to cheer Lori up with rhymes about one shoe off and one shoe on. She didn't think her brothers were very funny, but the tears stopped, until we arrived at church. When Clyde carried Lori from the car into the church and set her down, she burst into tears and headed straight for her Sunday school class.

It was embarrassing for Lori to go to church without a shoe, and at that moment I was upset. But later, after I reflected on it,

I was proud of Clyde for insisting that she go. It was a vivid example of how Clyde felt about attending church that followed the children throughout their lives. It also prompted me to always plan Lori's Sunday morning fashion ensemble on Saturday night, putting everything up high on a shelf.

There were lots of misadventures with the children getting to and from church. Our youngest son, Tim was always exploring and could amuse himself catching bugs, climbing trees or throwing stones in the lake. But sometimes that curious nature would result in some embarrassing situations.

One Sunday, after church, Clyde and I gathered the children together from the fellowship hall, piled them all into the car, said a few words of good bye to our friends and then we began our trip to the Tea Garden, our favorite Chinese Restaurant in downtown Grand Rapids. This was our regular after-church lunch treat, and the children looked forward to it each Sunday. About five miles from the church, I was reviewing the morning with the children who were all seated in the back seat.

"Mike, what did you like best about Sunday School today?" I started with our oldest. Mike, who was always conscious of being the role model for the younger ones replied, "The basketball player who spoke to our group."

"Oh, that's a good thought," I complimented him. I went on to our next child. "Andy," I continued, "What was your favorite part of this Sunday?"

"The chocolate chip cookies," Andy said with a grin.

Next I proceeded to our third child, "Lori, what was your favorite part of our morning?" I asked.

"The skit about Noah's ark," Lori said with a giggle. "I got to be a giraffe."

"Oh!" I said. "Sounds fun. Must be nice to be so tall. I'm sure you were a wonderful giraffe."

Clyde was chuckling at the children's responses as he drove the car and listened to the children.

So far I had basketball player, cookies and animals as the three best things about the morning. "Tim," I said to our youngest. "What was your favorite part of our morning?"

I braced myself, sure he'd have some crazy thing to tell me. But instead of Tim cracking a joke, there was total silence.

"Tim," I said again, a bit louder. "What was YOUR favorite thing about this morning?"

I waited; still no answer. I started to get a little irritated. I liked to joke with the children, but they were never allowed to just ignore me.

"Tim," I said once more. "Answer me please. What was your favorite thing this morning?"

When I didn't get a reply this time, I turned around in my seat to look at the back seat. There I saw three faces staring at me, and no Tim.

"Tim!" I shouted one more time, but Tim was not in the car! "Clyde!" I screamed. "Turn around, Tim isn't in the car!"

Then I yelled at the kids, "Why didn't the rest of you say something about Tim not being in the car with us?"

Three solemn faces with wide eyes starred at me. "He was out by the car with us when we were getting in the car," Mike said.

"There were some big boys playing in the parking lot," Andy said with a grin. "They probably chopped him in half and made him into corn flakes."

Lori puckered up ready to cry, when Mike assured her, "Don't worry, he'll turn up. We always find him sooner or later."

Clyde made a U turn in the middle of the road and sped back toward the church. We arrived to find everyone gone – except the janitor and Tim.

About a year later, our family was on vacation. We had everything piled into the car: luggage, ice chest, snack bag, sleeping bags, and all four of the kids crammed into the back seat. Clyde pulled into a little grocery store/gas station in a recreation area. He stopped at the gas pump and began pumping gas. Then he took the boys into the store with him. I took Lori to the restroom and met up with Clyde and the boys inside the store where we all picked out soft drinks, candy and bags of chips. Clyde paid for the gas and groceries, and we all climbed back into the car and headed on toward the lake.

A few miles down the road, Lori asked Tim a question. "Timmy, what kind of pop did you get?"

Tim didn't answer, so Lori asked him again, a bit louder this time, "Timmy! Answer me. I asked you nicely. What kind of pop did you get? Did you get root beer? I got Orange Crush. I might want to trade."

Again, Lori didn't get an answer.

Lori leaned over the front seat, "Tim!" she yelled. But Tim wasn't in the front seat between Clyde and me.

"Clyde!" I cried looking into the back seat. "We've lost Tim again!"

Clyde made another U turn in the road and raced back to the little grocery store. We found Tim sitting alone on the curb, sipping his chocolate Yahoo soda pop. He waved as Clyde drove into the parking area.

I jumped out of the car before Clyde even stopped and ran over to Tim. I grabbed him into a big hug and asked "Were you scared?"

"Nope," Tim said with a chocolate-tinted grin. "You always come back and get me."

SNAPSHOT 10

Pretty Little Blonde Hero

Vacation Bible School was an annual event that brought the children in the community to our country church in Michigan. It was at Vacation Bible School where I met Lauren, a pretty little

55

seven year old, with long blonde hair, big blue eyes and a shy smile. Lauren had been invited to VBS by another church member, and each day she arrived excited and enthusiastic to learn more about God. I didn't know anything about Lauren's family life, but I sensed a connection with this sweet little girl.

One of our Vacation Bible School games included incentives for children to attend each day. Vacation Bible School is exactly that – a week long Bible school during summer break from school. One of our incentives for attendance rewards that year involved a big jar of pennies. Children who attended every day of Vacation Bible School would receive perfect attendance certificates and the opportunity to reach into the penny jar and pull out as many pennies as they could hold in one grab.

Lauren seemed fascinated by this goal, and promised me that she would be there every day. At the time, I had no idea how deeply this reward reached this sweet little girl, or how it would anchor her faith. And so, I've asked Lauren to tell the rest of her story.

Lauren:

When I first came to Vacation Bible School, I remembered looking at Gerrie and thinking that she was the most glamorous woman I'd ever met. She was always dressed so fashionably, with her hair styled in the newest trend and she made me feel so special. My family was extremely poor, and we were actually living in a garage at the time; we didn't even have a bathroom. My father was an anti-government extremist who wouldn't pay taxes or let me or my brothers and sisters go to school. We had nothing, and when I heard Gerrie promise that I could have as many pennies as I could hold just for coming to Vacation Bible School every day, I thought that that was the coolest thing I could achieve.

I loved coming to church. Even though my mother and father didn't attend church or talk about God at home, I had accepted the Lord at age five at my Grandma's church, and I loved learning about God and serving God; and the connections I made at church were comforting. My family life was so dysfunctional that going to church was one outlet where I could see "normal" people.

Over the next few years, I attended Vacation Bible School at Gerrie's church several times, always because of Sue, our kind neighbor who would pick me up and take me home. I talked to God a lot about our family life, and I hung on every word from Pastor Clyde about how God loved me and had a plan for my life. By the time I was about 11, my father had formed a secret government of his own and had a small following of similarly-minded people. He bought a piece of property and we moved to a compound, with several families living on our property, all dedicated to the same anti-government philosophy.

I was far too young to understand the implications of the weapons my father marketed or other illegal trade he was involved in. But I was aware of the unusual cult environment we lived in and how very different my life was compared to the one I learned about at church.   When my father continued to become more extreme, my mother decided to divorce him. That's when my father loaded my four youngest siblings into the motor home, and headed for Florida where he had connections with more anti-government extremists.

My mom was reluctant to go through law enforcement to maintain custody of all of us children, since she was afraid that she would be held accountable for many of my father's crimes. Her greatest fear was that if she turned in my dad, the courts would take the children from her. At age 11, all I could do was pray that somehow God would rescue my family from this craziness.

My dad did allow us to see my mother, but it was a tiresome ritual of driving back and forth from Michigan to Florida every week. When I observed large sums of cash, jewelry and weapons peppered into our visits with Dad, I knew things were getting dangerous for all of us. Dad started talking about moving to Canada, and I didn't want to go, I just wanted to return to my mom. This resulted in a huge argument until finally he said, "If *you want to leave, just go! You can drive your grandmother back to Michigan."*

And so at age 11, I drove my grandmother's big old Lincoln town car from Florida to Michigan. I prayed all the way home that somehow God would keep us all safe. The first place I wanted to go was back to church where I could feel some sense of normalcy and peace. And I was done with visits to my father.

Eventually, things fell apart between my dad and his buddies in Florida and they had a huge disagreement. These were very bad guys, dealing in drugs and weapons and my father's life and the lives of my entire family were at risk. When things began to disintegrate between Dad and this gang of criminals he was working with in Florida, there was a shoot-out and Dad decided to go into hiding. In the dead of night, he loaded my younger siblings into the motor home and escaped to Canada. The gang from Florida was composed of desperate criminals; renegades who dealt in all sorts of illegal activity. My father owed them money, and they wanted to find him. They called our house all the time, demanding that we tell them where Dad was. They threatened us with horror stories of torture or feeding us to the alligators if we didn't tell them where to find my father. They always threatened to kill my siblings when they found Dad, if we didn't divulge Dad's location. All we could tell them was the truth – we did not know where my Dad was hiding.

The worst part of the threats was that these extremists knew where we lived and what our daily routine was. They told us things they couldn't have known if they hadn't been watching us. They continued to harass us frequently, making threats or suggesting they had carried out threats against my dad and siblings. My Dad would call occasionally with threats of violence as well. His mental condition was so unstable that he would spew vile phrases at us and said he would harm my siblings if we tried to find them. For over two years we didn't know where my younger siblings were or if they were dead or alive.

The people at church were wonderful and supported me and my mom through the struggle. I became heavily involved in church, and I felt strength and encouragement from Gerrie,

Pastor Clyde and many of the church leaders. I joined the youth group and continued to put my faith in God, rather than in law enforcement, as I prayed for the safety of my sister and brothers, my mom and myself.

My mother lost our home in a bank foreclosure, and we moved into a tiny 900 square foot house. My mom, sister and I continued to be harassed by Dad's former partners, and my mother became despondent over the loss of her children. Dad would call off and on with threats of his own. As God protected us, I clung to my faith, supported by all those wonderful people at church. The Lord gave me hope and the strength to encourage my older sister and my mother.

I was just a teenager, yet unwillingly, I was the spiritual leader in the household. I stayed in the word all through high school, finding wisdom in my Bible, and strength through my prayers and the prayers of others at church.

It was nearly five years after my siblings were taken by my dad when I graduated from high school. Dad had called a few times over the years, always careful to hang up within a minute to avoid having the call traced. He didn't ever let us talk to the kids. His calls were always evil prophesies or threats of injuring the children if anyone tried to find him. My mom was devastated and without hope, while I gripped my faith and continued to pray with the support of our church members. One of our church members was Trish, a social worker who knew me from the many visits she'd made to our home over the years when my father wouldn't let us go to school. She was married to Bob, a state police officer. The two of them had encouraged me and offered to help me find my brothers and sister.

One summer day just after graduation, my friend Kelly and I planned a big day of shopping at the mall in the city. Kelly drove over to my house to pick me up and as we were pulling out of my mom's driveway, I stopped her and said, "I'm sorry, Kelly. I've changed my mind. I don't want to go."

"Why?" she asked incredulously. We had both been looking forward to this trip.

"I don't know," I told her. "I just don't think I should go today."

Kelly pulled the car back into the driveway and turned off the ignition. I grabbed my purse and she and I both got out of the car and went into the house. The phone was ringing when I walked in the door. I picked up as I set my purse on the counter. "Hello?" I said.

It was Dad.

"Devil child," I heard his raspy, familiar voice. "You think you are protected from evilness; ha! You are evil! You'll never see your brothers and sisters again. Even if the police come, I will kill the kids before I'll ever give them up to the communists!"

I didn't know what to say. It was a familiar pattern, and I grew more fearful that if I said anything to make him angrier he might really do something harmful to the children. It had been almost five years since he'd taken the children from Mom, and each call confirmed my fears that his mental health continued to spiral downward.

I could hear my father's ragged breath as my heart pounded, wondering if I could somehow keep him on the phone long enough to trace the phone call when an operator's voice interrupted the call with "Please deposit 25 cents for the next three minutes."

My father shouted an explicative and hung up. I felt the familiar disappointment again, as I lost his connection, but then I noticed that the voice asking for the 25 cents didn't sound like a recording, it sounded like a live voice.

"Hello, Operator?" I asked hopefully.

"This is the operator. How can I help you?" came the reply.

I was stunned — it wasn't a recorded voice — this was a real person, and a real person might be able to help.

"Please don't hang up! Please don't hang up!" I cried. "That was my father and he has my brothers and sister. He kidnapped them almost five years ago! Please, please, please help me! He's going to kill them!"

The operator listened to me pour out my story and then said, "I believe you. Hold on, I need to get my supervisor."

A few seconds later another voice came over the line, and I told my story again, explaining the latest threat. "He said that if the police come to get the kids, he'll kill them all. Please tell me where this phone call came from."

The supervisor replied, "We never give out this kind of information," she said professionally. "I could lose my job for telling you that this call came from a phone booth in Brighton, Michigan."

"Can you call up there?" I gasped.

"Yes, hold tight, I'll call," She replied, and then I could hear the phone ring and ring, but no one answered. She gave me the phone number and the street address of the phone booth.

I thanked the operator and hung up the phone, with a flicker of hope in my heart. I called Gerrie and Pastor Clyde and they prayed with me, and then they invited our whole church to pray that this new clue might bring back the children to safety. Within hours, Gerrie had everyone from church praying.

I called Bob, my state police officer friend from church, who agreed to see what he could do with the new information. I felt restless and unable to sit around and wait for law enforcement protocol. I wanted to head up there to find them. My mom was so distressed, desperately concerned that my father would hurt the kids.

About two hours later, I decided on my own that I would call that number back. I thought I'd just see if anyone answered that pay phone in Brighton.

My hand shook as I dialed the number and listened as the phone rang and rang. Finally a girl's voice said, "Hello." I asked if she knew anything about a man with some children and a motor home, but she said she was just walking by.

A few minutes later, with continued resolve, I called again. The phone rang several times, when this time a man answered the phone. I jumped right in with my story, explaining that I was looking for an older abusive man with four kids who was driving a motor home.

To my surprise, the voice said, "I work in the laundry here and heard the phone ringing outside. I do know of an older man who comes in regularly to do laundry who has some kids. He acts very strange. But they aren't in a big motor home; this guy drives a blue van. I noticed the van because it has temporary license plates. He's an older guy with a girl and three boys, and I've always thought something wasn't quite right with them."

"Yes!" I cried. "That's them. Thank you."

I hung up the phone and immediately dialed Bob. "Don't look for the motor home; they are in a blue van with temporary plates. In Brighton," I told him.

Bob began to work with Michigan law enforcement to plan a rescue of the children. I was working on my own plan, completely directed by the Lord.

I knew that my Dad had set up a string of little businesses, all under alias names. So I began calling directory assistance, requesting a number in Brighton under the names I remembered Dad using. I tried them all, but each time I came up with nothing. I prayed, "Please Lord, help me find them," and sat with my head in my hands. And then I thought I would try to get the number under the name of Howard, the guy we thought was with my dad. And sure enough – this time the operator could find a number.

My dad has a very unique voice, and I knew that I could confirm his identity from hearing it over the phone. But I also knew that he would never talk to me if I called him. So Mom and I went to a neighbor's house where they had a telephone with two extensions. We had our neighbor call the number we received from the operator, while Mom listened in on one extension and I listened in on the other. Before he dialed the phone, our neighbor asked us, "Who should I ask for?"

Mom and I looked at each other and shrugged. I said, "Ask for Mary."

So our neighbor dialed the number and when a man answered with, "Hello," I knew immediately it was my father.

"Hello," our neighbor said, "Is Mary there?"

"No, sorry you must have the wrong number," my father said in his gravelly voice. "You're the third person to call for Mary today. I think she must have had this number before."

Mom and I were elated. Dad was right there in Michigan, in a house with a telephone, and I knew the number. And he wasn't even suspicious about the phone call we had placed since he'd been getting phone calls for Mary that day! All I needed was the street address. I dialed O for operator to try to glean critical information for rescuing my siblings.

"Can you give me an address for a phone number?" I asked the operator. I told her everything, from start to finish, crying and pleading my story. And then, contrary to company policy, she gave me the address.

I gave the information regarding the location to Bob, and together with Michigan State Police, he designed a plan to surprise my dad in the middle of the night. Since Dad had threatened many times that he would kill the children before he'd let the courts take them from him, the police thought a nighttime rescue would be the safest way to rescue the kids.

I called Gerrie, and she had everyone praying all night for us.

"It's going to happen at 3 a.m." I told Gerrie over the phone.

"Then we'll be praying from midnight until we hear from you," Gerrie told me. She organized a whole circle of people from church willing to stay up all night to pray for my siblings' safe return.

The people at the church weren't the only ones praying. I was talking to God constantly, asking Him to keep the kids safe and to bring them back to us. I was afraid to be too excited yet optimistic that this might be the beginning of the end of this ordeal. I wanted to go up there and be part of the rescue, but Bob insisted that I trust the police and their ability to handle this situation professionally. The plan was to surround the house, scope everything out and then send in a SWAT team. It should be over quickly, and they would bring the children back here to our house.

Kelly was there with me, and she and I prayed and prayed that night, watching the clock as the hours slowly slipped by. But 3 a.m. came, and we didn't hear anything. Then 4 a.m. came and still nothing. When it was 5 a.m. I called Bob, but he didn't answer.

Finally an Indiana State police car drove in the driveway around 6 a.m., but Bob didn't have the children. He got out of the car and said, "Lauren, I don't know how to tell you this, but they weren't there. There was nobody there."

My mother was crushed. I stood there in the early morning light feeling like the wind had been knocked out of me. This was really, really bad news. This was the closest we'd come to finding the kids in five years and yet nothing.

Kelly was still there beside me. She grabbed my arm, "Let's just drive up there," she said.

Fueled with my faith, and Kelly's encouragement, I got in her car and we just began driving northeast, toward Brighton, about 75 miles from our house, looking for a blue van. It was a shot in the dark at best, but it was better than sitting around doing nothing.

A few miles from Brighton, we drove through a tiny little town called Hell, Michigan. I had been watching the driveways, side roads and parking lots the entire trip, hoping and praying for a glimpse of a blue van. As Kelly slowed down to drive through Hell, I looked at a small house, and to my astonishment, I saw my brother David, playing with a goat beside my father's big bus. God had put me right on the very road where my father had the kids!

Kelly drove to the nearest grocery store, where I called the police. Within minutes, a patrol car drove in the lot, and a policeman gathered information to begin a plan to rescue my siblings. While we were sitting there, a blue van went by and I recognized the driver as Howard, the scary guy who worked for my dad; and to my amazement, my two brothers were passengers in the van.

"That's him!" I cried. "That's the guy who works for my dad. And those two boys are my brothers!"

The police officer hopped into his patrol car and pulled the van over a few miles down the road. Howard was handcuffed and taken into police custody. My two younger brothers had been brainwashed by my Dad for almost five years that they would be killed or mistreated if the police ever captured them.

These two boys became so terrified, one passed out and the other went into shock. It was terrible to see them, and not be able to go to them and comfort them, but at the same time it was a jubilant victory because I could see that they were finally safe.

By now there were about 20 police cars swarming the area. The police had us pull into a church parking lot nearby and wait. Quickly they surrounded the house where I had seen David and demanded that my father release David and my sister Grace. Grace was in the bathtub at the time of the raid, and she came outside wrapped in a bath robe. David was in the house ready to fight to save my father. David's brainwashing by my father was so intense that police actually had to handcuff him to bring him to safety. My dad barricaded himself in the bedroom and police used tear gas to finally get him out.

Kelly drove me to the police station where we were able to see my three brothers and little sister for the first time in nearly five years. The last time I saw Grace, she was a little girl, and now, she was a lanky 5' 10" teenager. She and my oldest brother David were fearful, but yet they looked relieved to be in police custody. My two youngest brothers had been so isolated from social contact, they barely spoke and what they did say was very hard to understand. They were terrified of what was to come.

Later that day, all four of the children piled into Kelly's tiny little car, and we all went home to begin the process of rebuilding our lives together. The church was there to celebrate with us, offering everything from clothing to new beds for them. The kids had to go through a great deal of deprogramming and counseling, and catching up in school was a challenge. I stayed with my Mom for a full year to help our family mend from the scars of their five year ordeal. And all that time, God was there to sustain us all. Even today, I still thank Him for hearing my prayer and bringing our family back together.

Lauren's story doesn't end here. While she was in the midst of the turmoil of not knowing if her three brothers and little sister were dead or alive, Lauren was trying hard to be a normal teenager. Lauren focused a lot of her attention and energy at our church, where she was active in our youth group, worship and prayer group.

When Lauren was 15, her siblings had been missing about a year. The principal at her school knew about the situation with her family, and wanted to do something to help. The principal's daughter was working for Campus Crusade. She told her father that the upcoming Campus Crusade conference might be a wonderful opportunity and comfort to Lauren. When the principal and his daughter invited Lauren to attend the conference, she politely declined. The conference was scheduled right around Christmas, and Lauren's absence at home would be hard for her mother.

"Thank you," Lauren told her them. "But no, we don't have the money to attend."

"That's not a problem, your conference fees have already been paid," was the principal's reply.

"But I don't have the money for the transportation costs," Lauren said, certain that she would not be attending the big event.

"Your bus fare is paid too," said the principal's daughter, with a gleam in her eye. "Both ways."

Reluctantly, Lauren agreed to go to the Campus Crusade conference, almost against her will. The plan was for her to ride to Kansas City on a chartered bus. The day Lauren left for the conference, it was a cold, gloomy day and Lauren was alone. She didn't know anyone on the trip, and she was deeply concerned about leaving her mother behind at Christmastime.

Shyly, this young teenager got on the bus and sat down next to a stranger. As she looked out the window, tears of grief filled her eyes and she tried to hide them. Lauren was sure her first inclination had been right. She did not want to be on this trip.

Just as the bus driver was about to close the door to the bus, a college-aged man boarded. He was tall, athletic, devastatingly handsome and very tan, something that stands out in December in the Midwest. Instead of luggage, the young man had his clothes tossed over his shoulder in a black garbage bag. Lauren took one look at him through her tears and said to the passenger next to her, "That's the man I'm going to marry."

Mortified that she had blurted something so silly out loud, Lauren sniffled in embarrassment. "I don't know why I said that," she confessed to her seatmate, "I don't even know that person."

The passenger next to her said, "Don't you know who that is? That's Jeff Stackhouse. He's a famous basketball player from Florida."

Jeff took the seat right behind Lauren and struck up a conversation with the college-aged passenger next to him. Lauren was still disillusioned with the trip, but she was impressed with the discussion going on behind her. Jeff was talking about the book of Romans with his seat mate.

"I remember him talking with such conviction," Lauren recalls. "I'd never heard anyone talk about a book in the Bible like that." As the bus wheels hummed on down the highway through the rain and slush on the road, Lauren was comforted by Jeff's voice that continued the conversation about Romans throughout the night.

The Campus Crusade conference was huge, with around 30,000 high school and college-aged participants. There were dozens of activities and events and Lauren met many interesting participants. But she thought it odd that with all the activities, she didn't see any of her new friends twice - except Jeff. It seemed that she kept bumping into him throughout the conference, and he was always accompanied by the same girl with orange hair. Lauren began to relax and enjoy the conference and discovered a whole week of activity filled with many encouraging people.

When the conference was over, several busses were dispatched for the return trip. When Lauren got to the loading area, she boarded the first bus she found headed for Michigan. As she entered the bus, she didn't notice a big foot in the aisle until she stumbled over it. It was Jeff!

He grinned at her and said, "Did you have a nice trip?"

Lauren laughed in embarrassment and then sat down in the seat next to him, and she and Jeff chatted all the way home. She learned that Jeff was visiting his parents during Christmas break from college. Lauren and Jeff discovered that they had many things in common. Jeff asked about Lauren's life, and she shared that she was from a small town in Indiana. Jeff chuckled because he had grown up in another small town, just five miles from Lauren's home town. At the end of the bus ride, Lauren and Jeff exchanged contact information, and he wrote to Lauren later from college, encouraging her and offering her spiritual guidance. In summer, Jeff came home from college to work for local basketball camps, and he continued to encourage Lauren in her family's crisis.

When Lauren graduated from high school, her relationship with Jeff changed. Lauren was no longer a shy teenager, but a confident, young woman of God. She and Jeff fell in love and a year after her siblings were found, Lauren married Jeff.

Lauren and Jeff have been happily married for over 25 years and have been faithfully serving the Lord their entire marriage. My husband Clyde was privileged to serve on Jeff's ordination board when Jeff became a pastor. Lauren is one of the most beautiful women I know. She and Jeff have two handsome sons that continue their family legacy. From that tiny little wide-eyed blonde in Vacation Bible School so many years ago, to a daring rescue coordinator as a teenager, to a pastor's wife as an adult, Lauren continues to inspire others with her strength of character, always putting her faith into action.

SNAPSHOT 11

Then Came Grant

When my children were in grade school, one of my favorite events was the annual Gull Lake Bible Conference about 60 miles north of our home. One year I decided to take Lori and Tim, the youngest of our four children with me, since there were plenty of activities planned for children at the conference.

I thought that Clyde would be fine looking after our two oldest children, Andy and Mike, back at home in my absence. And he was – for awhile. Until the second day when on their way into town, Clyde found a man along side the road with a broken-down motorcycle.

The motorcyclist looked like the character Jim Bronson in the television show, "Then Came Bronson." He was a tough, edgy vagabond, dressed in dark leather jeans and jacket and a sweaty wool hat. He had a cigarette hanging out of the corner of his mouth and a defiant swagger as he walked up to the car when Clyde pulled over. His hands were covered in grease from trying to repair his Harley Davidson, but Clyde still offered his hand in greeting as he introduced himself.

"How ya doing?" Clyde asked extending his hand. "I'm Clyde Mills, pastor of the church up the road. It looks like you need a little help."

The man grasped Clyde's hand and said, "Thanks. Grant Hadley. Broken fuel line." He nodded toward the shiny red motorcycle.

"We might be able to load the bike in the back of the station wagon," Clyde said. "Can you fix it?"

Grant nodded. "Need parts."

"Okay then," Clyde said. He walked to the back of the station wagon, folded the seats down, and the two men loaded the bike. Andy and Mike were wide-eyed as the unwashed smell of Mr. Hadley filled the front seat of the car.

Clyde drove back to our house where he and Grant unloaded the bike and pushed it into our garage. Andy and Mike were underfoot, watching their father in action, wondering what would happen next with this new, larger-than-life character. Clyde got out a tool box and told Grant he was welcome to use any tools in the garage. Then he took Mike and Andy into the house where he fixed a sandwich for the stranger and brought it out to the garage. Mike grabbed a bottle of root beer and both he and Andy followed their father to take care of their visitor.

At the end of the day, Grant had the bike in pieces, all scattered around the garage. When Clyde drove Grant into town to get the part he needed, they found out it had to be ordered and would arrive the next day. So Clyde did the only logical thing he could think of to solve the problem of where Grant would wait for his part to arrive. Clyde invited Grant to spend the night at our house.

Grant began to relax with Clyde, Andy and Mike. He showered, washed his clothes, ate dinner with the family and helped clean up after. He watched television with the boys and gratefully accepted a clean bed to sleep in at bedtime. It took all day the next day to repair the bike, and by sundown, the boys had invited Grant to spend the night at our house again.

By now Grant had warmed up to the family and stopped talking in one-word grunts. Grant told stories of his adventures touring the country on the motorcycle. He explained to the boys that he was on his way to Mexico when his bike broke down. In two short days Mike and Andy had begun to think of Grant as a sort of folk hero. Clyde, however, saw a sad, lonely soul.

Clyde asked Grant about his faith, kindly inquiring about what Grant believed about God and asking if he had any questions. A thoughtful discussion ensued and Clyde asked, "Do you believe that Jesus is your savior?" Grant nodded. "Have you ever asked Jesus to come into your heart to be Lord of your life?"

"No, sir," Grant said. "I have not."

"Would you like to?" Clyde asked.

Grant nodded.

And then Clyde and Grant prayed the prayer that so many others have, "Dear Lord Jesus, I invite You to become my Savior and Lord and to reign in my heart forever." Grant looked up and it was the first time Clyde had seen him smile.

The next day, over another of Clyde's breakfasts, Clyde explained that he was taking Andy and Mike up to Gull Lake to meet me and our other two children for a vacation. Grant nodded in his gruff way and began gathering his things into his duffle bag, preparing to begin his next adventure.

Clyde and the boys got into the car, prepared to wave good bye, when to their surprise instead of fastening the duffle bag to the Harley Davidson, Grant threw his bag into the back of the station wagon and climbed into the back seat of our car. Clyde looked at the boys and smiled then started the car to head north.

When Clyde arrived with the older children, I expected the boys to be wearing mismatched socks or T-shirts inside out. But I didn't expect them to be in the company of a dangerous outlaw, and that's just what Mr. Grant Hadley looked like to me. I was always glad to meet someone new, but I was nervous about this character and his influence on my children.

"How could you pick this guy up?" I asked incredulously. "He looks like a gangster."

"He's not so bad," Clyde assured me. "He played with Mike and Andy, helped out with chores and even made his bed this morning."

"Made his bed?" I cried. "How do you know that?"

"He slept in Tim's room," Clyde said. "I noticed that the bed was made this morning."

"He slept at our house?" I was horrified. The thought of that greasy hair on Tim's powder blue pillow case was making my skin crawl. "He looks like a Hell's Angel! He could have murdered you in your sleep."

Clyde grinned. "Gerrie, he wasn't going to harm us. He needed help." Clyde gave me his 'warming me up hug' to assure me. "He accepted the Lord last night."

That took some of the wind out of my argument, but I still wanted more information.

"So why is he here?" I asked.

"I'm not sure," Clyde admitted. "When we left to come on up here, Grant just got in the car and came along."

"So he thinks he's going on vacation with us?" I gasped, taking in the black leather jeans and jacket, scruffy beard, shaggy red hair and air of rebellious arrogance. He was about as opposite of our lifestyle as you could get.

Clyde shrugged his shoulders. "Gerrie," he leaned forward and whispered in my ear. "He is on vacation with us."

My eyes got really wide, and I was about to tell Clyde that we were not going to take a stranger with us on our vacation when Mike piped up. "Dad, since Mr. Hadley already accepted the Lord, Mom wants him to hit the road."

About that time Phil, the college-aged Bible conference leader came over and introduced himself to Grant and proceeded to invite Grant to a group activity. Professionally, Phil worked with the State probation office. He was watching Grant carefully. After an hour or two, Clyde found Grant, and they decided to return home. Grant was ready to get back on his motorcycle and head south to Mexico.

"Clyde," Phil said to Clyde quietly as Grant was climbing into our car. "Grant is under the influence of drugs."

"It's okay," Clyde said. "He'll be leaving in the morning."

Clyde and Grant got into our car and headed back to our home. Clyde let Grant stay overnight a third night in Tim's bed. The next day, Grant headed for Mexico and Clyde returned to the Bible conference where we continued a nice vacation at Gull Lake. We never heard from Grant again, but I have often reflected on how God put Clyde in that young man's path to fix the motorcycle, introduce him to God, and treat him to our family vacation.

SNAPSHOT 12

A Child's Prayer

Welcome To

Social Security

ROSEVILLE CA

Your ticket number is

A11!

Thank you. Please wait
to be called. Try using
our online services at
www.socialsecurity.gov

7/12/2013 09:28:48 AM

When pastoring in a farming community, you learn quickly that much of the culture is driven by the farming calendar. There's planting season, growing season and harvest. Each season requires different duties from the farmer, but the commitment required remains the same. Children who grow up on a farm learn early on that farming is an unforgiving occupation and the crops are a priority for the family.

There was a little boy in our church named Gene who played in the school band. He was a talented little musician and practiced his trumpet faithfully until he became a proficient trumpeter. When the teacher scheduled a spring concert on a Saturday afternoon, she had no idea that many of the parents would be unable to attend because it was planting season.

Gene took the concert invitation home to his family. "I sure hope you'll be there, Dad," Gene said eagerly. "Everyone will be there to hear me play."

Gene's father looked at the date for the concert and then out at the fields ready for seed. He put the invitation down on the table and said quietly to his son, "Gene, I would love to attend your concert. But this is scheduled for next week, right when I'll be planting the corn. There is just no way that I can leave the farm then."

"But Dad," Gene begged, "It's just for a few hours. Surely you can come just for an hour or two to hear me play."

Gene's father shook his head. "Son, I only have a few days to get the seed sown. It would be completely irresponsible for me to neglect the planting for our farm just to attend a band concert."

"But Dad," Gene persisted. "Isn't there any way you can come?"

"Not unless it rains," said his father.

So Gene decided to pray for rain. Gene's young faith was so strong. Clyde had led him to the Lord as a small child and Gene was a regular in church and Sunday school. He knew that God loved him and that God answered prayers. So Gene prayed and prayed that it would rain so his dad could go to the concert.

The day of the concert arrived, bright and sunny. Gene's dad took the planting equipment out to the field. But just before the concert was scheduled to begin, dark clouds gathered and with a flash of lightning and a clap of thunder, it began to rain. It went from a small sprinkle to a pelting downpour.

Gene's father returned to the machine shed with the planting equipment, changed his clothes and headed to the school to attend the concert.

Gene saw his father in the crowd, grinned at his Dad and gave a tiny finger wave. When it was time for the concert to begin, the small boy took a deep breath, pressed his trumpet to his lips and played beautifully. Gene's father was touched by the music and looked around at the crowd to see if they were impressed with his son's playing as well.

To Gene's father's surprise, none of the other farmers were in the audience. During the next week, Gene's father asked the other farmers about the rainstorm only to discover that none of them had experienced any rain on that Saturday. Gene's father began to realize that the surprise cloud burst was isolated to their farm and the one next door. The downpour had brought all planting to a stop, but only on two farms in the whole county. On Gene's father's fields, there was indeed too much rain to plant seed, but the rest of the community didn't get a drop.

Gene believed God answered his prayer that day. That little boy's faith grew, just like the corn growing in his father's fields. Gene was faithful to the Lord as he matured into adulthood. He became a very successful businessman, who serves in numerous areas of ministry and continues to pray every day.

SNAPSHOT 13

Adapting To The Situation:
My Short-Lived Career as an Athlete

I have been called into roles all my life where I had no experience or reference point. I went from living an urban lifestyle to living in a rural community, often wishing there was a user's manual for understanding the different culture. As a pastor's wife, I've taken on administrative roles, coordinated major events, been a keynote conference speaker and taught Bible studies. Whenever something needed doing, if Clyde couldn't find someone else, I was the designated volunteer. Every morning I pray for God to use me for His purposes, and I draw on that prayer when I need to be adaptable.

I thought I had my adaptability well-honed until the day I was asked to substitute as a player on our church's women's softball team. I had gone out to the game, prepared to watch and cheer, even though I had no idea what the rules were or how to keep score. I just went to the game to support the women on our team and because I liked the fellowship in the stands. I thought I'd made a significant contribution to the team when I designed their uniforms. But I had rarely played sports as a child and the rules of softball escaped me. That ball seemed pretty hard to me to be considered "soft" and even after years of watching Clyde and the kids play, I never knew how many minutes were in an inning.

Our church's women's softball team was very successful. In fact, they were undefeated in the league, and Clyde was their coach. I was so proud of how sharp they looked in their tomboy feminine uniforms. The girls wore hot pink shorts and black t shirts with the church logo in hot pink lettering. They also wore big pink bows in their hair.

It was a warm summer afternoon when I drove over to a nearby ball park to watch our team play an away game. I arrived as the game was about to begin, and just as I settled into a seat in the bleachers, Michelle ran up to me and said, "Mom! I'm so glad you're here."

"I'm glad to be here too sweetie," I said to her, hugging her hello. "Good luck! Score a lot of points."

"We need your help," Michelle said and tugged at my arm. "We're one girl short, and we need you to sub. Our team just had a meeting, and we decided to have you sub for our missing player until she gets here."

"But I don't play softball," I said in protest. "I haven't played since. . ." I thought for a second, "well, probably sixth grade." Chilling childhood memories came flooding back of always being the last one chosen for a baseball team. I was the last and the least for a good reason!

Michelle wouldn't take no for an answer. "That doesn't matter. Come on!" She persisted. "The game is going to start, and we'll have to forfeit the game if we don't have enough players."

"Okay," I stood up, gathering my purse, my book, my transistor radio and my chocolate. "Where do I play?"

"Right field," Michelle said, picking up my ice chest. "You'll have to put all this stuff in the dugout. Come on."

"What do I do?" I asked as I tucked my things under a bench. Clyde and Michelle began giving me instructions at the same time.

"Nothing, just stand there," Clyde said. "No one ever hits anything into right field."

"What do I do if a ball does come out there?" I asked doubtfully.

Michelle answered, "Just catch it, and as fast as you can, throw it back to home plate."

"Which one is home plate?" I asked.

"The one where the batter is standing at," Tim, Clyde's assistant coach, said as he handed me a softball mitt and pointed toward right field.

My white tennis shoes rippled through the grass of the softball field as I walked out to where Tim had pointed. I couldn't figure out how to put the mitt on my hand. It seemed like it must be for a left-hander, because I couldn't get my right hand into the fingers, so I set it down on the grass once I arrived at my "right field" destination.

"I think I'm actually in wrong field," I said to myself.

It was boring out there in the right field. I didn't have anyone to talk to, and I couldn't see what was going on between the pitcher and the batter. I didn't know if the other team was scoring any points or not, but I was ready if any of those not-so-

soft balls came my way. My plan was to get out of the way first, let the ball hit the ground and then capture it to throw to Homer's plate.

The sun was shining, and it was getting a little hot out there. I wondered if I could call a time out, so I could go back to the dugout and get a soft drink and some sunscreen. I put my hand up to shade my eyes and prayed that nothing requiring my athletic ability would happen. I had just about decided that playing right field was not very exciting when I heard the crack of a bat and a ball went sailing out to my left and into the trees that lined the field.

"Foul ball!" the umpire shouted angrily.

I didn't know what to do! But then I heard Cathy yell, "Run Mom! Get the ball!" And then all the kids started yelling, "Go Mom! Run!"

I turned around and went racing after the ball. My white tennis shoes were getting grass-stained, but I ran as fast as I could, off the field and into the weeds, bushes and trees that bordered the field. This was my chance to prove to my children that all their athletic ability didn't just come from their father.

I wasn't sure where the ball had landed, but I had a general idea, so I began walking through the grass and the bushes, searching for that softball. I knew it was white and if I kept looking in this small area, I was bound to find it. Sure enough, there it was, nestled under a milkweed plant. I grabbed it and ran back to the field as fast as my now green-striped tennis shoes would take me.

"I found it!" I yelled waving the ball in the air.

"Throw the ball!" Tim yelled. "Throw it home!"

"Throw it Mom!" They all yelled from the bench. "Throw it home! Throw it! Throw hard!" They were all laughing uncontrollably, but cheering me on just the same.

I wound up and threw the ball as far as I could. It dropped just short of the second baseman, who scooped it up and threw it to the pitcher. I was so proud of my play.

Tim walked out to the field with the regular right fielder who had just arrived. I gave her my mitt and jubilantly celebrated my amazing recovery of the softball.

"Do we get any points for finding the ball?" I asked, smoothing my hair and checking to see if I still had both earrings.

"Mom, they are called runs in softball, not points," Tim said patiently.

"Well, did we get any runs for it?" I persisted.

"No Mom," Tim explained. "It was a foul ball. The batter couldn't score on it. You didn't even have to go get it."

I was so disappointed, and I realized that the kids had all enjoyed a good laugh at my expense while I filled in as a substitute softball player. But I took solace in knowing that I had helped the kids get the game started. It was an opportunity God had presented for me to take a risk outside of my comfort zone, and I had accepted it. I was proud of that. (Mostly I was relieved that I didn't have to play right field anymore.)

Clyde was so proud of me and had high hopes that I might develop into a real softball player. I had shown great promise with my enthusiasm, effort and ability to take direction in the field. He went out and bought me a brand new softball mitt. I returned it the next day for some sparkly earrings and a bracelet to match. Later, as I reflected on the game, I realized that while my play of valiantly retrieving the softball might not have scored any points, it still contributed to the team. Softballs cost about $3 each, and that's too much money to just leave lying in the woods.

SNAPSHOT 14

The Short Cut Fight

Clyde and I have enjoyed more than 58 years of marriage, and he still makes my heart flutter whenever he enters a room. But we have conflicts in our lives, just like all married couples. In fact, occasionally we fight. I remember vividly one of the worst fights we ever had when our daughter Lori was about to give birth to her first child.

Lori was living in High Point, North Carolina. Clyde and I lived in Quincy, Michigan, a distance of about 700 miles. I was already terribly nervous about Lori's delivery, since just a few months earlier, our daughter-in-law Cathy had gone through a terrible 32 hour delivery before our first granddaughter was born. I was in constant prayer for Lori, asking God to watch over my little girl as well as her unborn baby. I have a lot of faith, but I still worry. So when Lori's husband, Mark, called and told us that Lori had gone into labor and that it was time for us to head to North Carolina, I was filled with anticipation of more labor and delivery drama. I tried not to be fretful and continued to pray that God would watch over Lori and the baby. It didn't occur to me to pray about getting to the hospital to be there with her.

I had already packed our suitcases. I grabbed our toothbrushes and Clyde and I jumped in the car and headed for North Carolina. By my calculations, if we didn't stop for anything more than gas, we could be at Lori's side in about 12 hours. I had a whole bag of snacks packed, so I was confident that we would be at Lori's side by nightfall. Clyde was driving our new car, and I was his navigator in the passenger seat, with a Triple A map in my lap. I was excited when we crossed the Michigan state border into Ohio earlier than I had expected. Perhaps we could get there in less than 12 hours!

Looking at my map, I thought we would drive east toward Akron and then south to North Carolina. But Clyde continued south toward Columbus.

"Clyde," I said, looking at my map. "The map seems to indicate that the best route would be to go east to Akron first and then south on Interstate 77."

"We're going south to Columbus," Clyde said, like the captain of the ship. "We'll head east after we go through Columbus. It's a much better route."

I looked at my map, noting that the main freeways were highlighted in red, while the smaller highways were printed in yellow. It seemed to me that we should be on the red roads, since freeways were bound to be our fastest route. But Clyde was driving, so I kept quiet about it and focused on my constant thoughts and prayers for Lori. Before long, we were just outside of Columbus. Clyde pulled over, and I ran to a pay phone to call Mark and see how Lori was doing.

"She's having some trouble, Mom," Mark said. "Please pray. I hope you and Dad can get here soon. Lori really wants you here."

I ran back to the car and told Clyde Mark's message. "We need to just keep moving," I told him. "The sooner we get there, the better."

Clyde nodded. He put the car in gear and headed back down the road. A few miles later, Clyde made a turn that took us into downtown Columbus.

I looked at my map and then at my watch, thinking of Lori at the hospital, and wanting to be there with her so badly. "Don't you think we should take the bypass?" I asked him, looking at the map in my lap. "It's rush hour. There's bound to be traffic."

"No," Clyde said at the wheel. "We'll make better time driving through the city, even if it is rush hour."

Before long, we were stuck in bumper to bumper traffic, sitting through two or three stop lights before moving one car-length forward and crawling through downtown Columbus.

I looked at my watch again, noting that we had traveled about six blocks in the past half hour and then thinking of Lori, in labor at the hospital. "We should have taken the bypass," I sighed. "We would have been past Columbus by now." I used a not-so-nice tone.

"Don't worry," Clyde said. "When we get out of this traffic, I know a short cut."

"I hope so," I said, polishing off the very last snack I had packed. I was so nervous in the terrible traffic, that I didn't even realize I had eaten every snack I had packed for the trip. Clyde was being stubborn, and it really irked me. I wasn't in a prayerful mood anymore.

I looked at the map. "Oh, I see, we'll just take Interstate 70 east and then go south on Interstate freeway 77," I said as I relaxed. I could see the red highlights on my map again. Once we got onto Interstate 77, I knew it was all freeway.

"No, I'm taking a better route," Clyde said, as he ran a yellow light in the gridlock, with car horns honking at him.

We finally made it through downtown Columbus, and I saw the sign pointing us toward I77. "There's the exit," I pointed to Clyde. But he drove right past it.

"What are you doing?" I cried, weary from being stuck in traffic so long. "The freeway exit is back there!"

"I told you; I know a short cut," Clyde said tartly.

"But the map shows. . ." I looked at the map again carefully to read the proper road sign names.

"Never mind the map," Clyde said, his voice a bit louder than necessary.

Clyde kept driving south, and soon we were traveling along a highway into the countryside. I knew we were going south, but I couldn't quite figure out which road. I kept looking for crossroads, trying to determine where we were on my map. The line on my map wasn't colored yellow anymore, just a tiny gray line with no name on it. We came to a little town.

"Shall we stop for dinner?" Clyde asked me as he pulled over.

"Dinner?!" I exclaimed. Dinner was about the last thing I wanted. The only thing on my mind or stomach was Lori. There was a pay phone within sight, so I jumped out of the car and raced to the phone to call and check on Lori.

"Things aren't going well," Mark told me. "She's in a lot of pain but not making much progress toward delivery."

"We're on our way," I told Mark. "We'll try to be there tonight."

I hung up the phone and ran back to the car. "I think we should turn around and get back on the freeway," I said to Clyde. "Lori needs us, and we are not going to get there tonight on this road."

"This road goes through," Clyde said confidently. "I told you it was a short cut."

So Clyde continued south on that road I couldn't name. Another hour went by, and I felt my stomach rumble. It was well past dinner time, but I didn't care. I just wanted to hurry up and get to Lori. We came to a small country store and Clyde pulled into the parking lot.

"I'm hungry," Clyde said. "I wonder where the restaurant is in this town."

I looked around. This was not a town. It was a tiny grocery store with one gas pump out front. I ran to find a phone, but they didn't have one. They didn't even have a restroom! Clyde filled up the car with gas, ran in to the store to pay for it, and came back with two stale candy bars and two bottles of warm Coke.

"This will have to do until we find a nice restaurant," he said cheerfully, handing me a chocolate bar and a Coke. He started the car and we continued down the country road.

I was getting angry. It made no sense to keep wandering around in the countryside. We needed to get back on the main road and connect to the freeway if we had any hope of seeing Lori that night.

Later that evening, Clyde pulled into a tiny little gas station to fill up the car. Across the street there was a small diner. "Should we stop for dinner?" Clyde asked innocently.

I didn't want to stop. I wanted to get to the hospital to check on Lori, but I kept my mouth shut about that. We went into the Greasy Spoon diner, ordered our meals and were back on the country road in no time.

After about an hour, the road became even narrower and we began to climb into the hills. According to my map, we were somewhere in the hills of West Virginia. I began to notice many ramshackle houses with various wrecked cars sprinkled about the landscape. I also noticed that a lot of these homes had outhouses out back.

"Clyde," I said. "I think we're on the wrong road. The crooked gray line on my map has ended. This road isn't even on my map."

About that time, Clyde made a left turn, up a narrow, bumpy road that curved around a big tree. Our car lurched into low gear as it began to climb a lengthy hill into the Appalachian Mountains. For hours we climbed deeper into the rugged terrain, up and down hills, around hairpin turns and down a washboard roadbed.

"Clyde," I said, looking at my map again. "We are lost."

"No, we're not," Clyde said. "This road will come out near the highway."

I kept thinking about Lori and getting more and more angry. Lori had asked me to be by her side, and even though she was a grown woman, about to give birth, she was my little girl! She needed me! And here I was, lost in Moonshine Country because Clyde was too stubborn to admit that he was lost.

"We are not going to come out near the highway. We are lost in these hills. There's not even any place to ask for directions!" I screamed, as my fury overflowed into tears. I was so angry and upset I couldn't even pray about this crazy situation.

"Well, I don't see why there isn't a motel around here, or a nice restaurant," Clyde replied calmly. "It's dark. We need to find a place to stay for the night."

"A motel?! A nice restaurant?!" I shouted. "There isn't even a decent place to wash your hands on this route! We can't stay overnight anywhere up here! We have to get back to the freeway!"

Clyde continued to drive through the narrow, winding roads, dodging the wildlife, rocks, branches and debris. By morning, we were both exhausted, he from driving and me from anger. As the hills became less steep, I could see the sunrise ahead, which indicated to me that we were indeed headed east. We continued downhill until eventually we did come out on a main highway somewhere near the North Carolina border.

By the time we arrived at the hospital, Lori had delivered a beautiful baby boy, by Cesarean Section, and was resting comfortably. God had answered my prayer about protecting my daughter and her new baby. She hadn't been alone. Mark, of course was there with her, but the pastor of their church stayed right there with her too, substituting as her father while Clyde wandered up and down backwoods country on his shortcut. Lori was exhausted, but happy, and best of all, the baby was perfect.

I was furious with Clyde for being so stubborn and unwilling to admit he was lost. Even today, he insists that we weren't lost and that he knew exactly where we were the entire trip. But our 12 hour trip took us 26 hours, more than twice as long as I had predicted with my map. And, it took me a bit longer than that to forgive Clyde for taking his short cut on such an important day.

Today we have a GPS to guide us, and now Clyde has two voices telling him which way is the quickest, most direct route. I still keep a map under the passenger seat in our car, and I always remember to pray for God's guidance whenever we start out on a road trip.

SNAPSHOT 15

Grow A Notch In Faith

When Michelle married my son Tim, I thought she was the best thing that could ever happen to him. She was young but had an enormous heart for the Lord. And I loved to watch her grow in faith.

Michelle:

One of the best lessons I learned from Mom early in our relationship was to grow in faith by notches. She taught me to recognize God working in my life in the big ways and the little ways. With each incident, my faith grew another notch. I recall a day when my faith grew several notches.

Tim and I were living in Michigan, and Mom had flown in from Florida to be a guest speaker at a women's conference in Upper Michigan. A few days before the trip, Mom's hearing aid needed repair, so she had the audiologist ship the hearing aid directly to our house. But by the morning of the conference, the hearing aid still hadn't arrived. We confirmed that it had been shipped, but FedEx had not delivered it by the time we had to leave for the conference.

"We have to leave now," I told Mom. "You'll be late for the conference if we don't get on the road." It was about four hours of travel in the car ahead of us, and we were going with a group of women, traveling in several cars.

That morning Dad had called from Florida, and Mom had all of us stand around the phone for him to pray with us. Dad had asked for safe travel and a successful conference. I still remember that he also prayed that each of us attending the conference would grow a notch in faith. Before he hung up Mom piped up with, "And please help my hearing aid to be delivered!"

We were all loaded in the cars, ready to go, when Mom asked one more time for a brief word with God. "Father, please get that hearing aid delivered, somehow. It will be nearly impossible for me to speak, answer questions or counsel the women at the conference if I can't hear."

My sister-in-law, Ellen, put the car in gear and we headed off for our long drive. Traveling through the beautiful countryside of Michigan, we were about 20 miles down the road when Ellen slowed the car down as we came to a little town. Mom spotted a McDonald's Golden Arches sign.

"Stop!" Mom chirped. "I need a diet coke."

Ellen slowed down, put on her turn signal and pulled into the parking lot just as I saw a FedEx truck with his signal light on, ready to pull out of the parking lot and back onto the highway.

"Stop that truck!" Mom shouted. "That's a FedEx truck and my hearing aids were shipped FedEx. He has my hearing aids! I just know it!"

I looked at Mom who was so eager to run over to a random delivery truck in faith along highway I-94. I thought she had gone crazy. Ellen was looking for a parking spot. Mom grinned at me in anticipation. "You just never know," she said with a twinkle in her eye and flew out of the car before Ellen even stopped.

"Stop! Stop!" Mom ran toward the FedEx truck in her high heels, waving her hands in the air. "I need my hearing aid!"
The FedEx driver stopped and timidly opened his window. Mom was gasping for breath, holding her side and leaning on the side of the truck.

"Do you have a package for Gerrie Mills?" she said between gulps of oxygen.

The driver grabbed his clipboard and asked her briskly, "What's your address?"

Mom didn't know our mailing address. "I don't know!" She cried. "Hold on, I'll find out."

Mom ran back to our car in a flurry, yanked open the car door and asked me, "What's my address?"

I was watching this whole scene unfold and laughing at how funny it was, "Mom, I'm not sure what your address is."

"No, no, no," She said, waving her hands and catching her breath. "I mean, what's YOUR address, the address where I had them ship the hearing aid?"

I rattled off my home address. Mom slammed the car door and ran back to the FedEx truck.

I watched her talk more with the FedEx driver. "You don't really think..." I said to Ellen and the other passengers. "We're 30 miles from home. You can't just stop random FedEx trucks on a freeway to find your missing package, can you?"

In disbelief I watched the FedEx driver hand a clipboard to Mom. She scribbled her signature and then he gave her a small white box.

Mom ran back to the car waving the box in the air triumphantly. I was stunned at how impossibly God had just delivered Mom's hearing aid. She climbed back in the car, and as Ellen pulled back on to the highway, Mom tore open the package and popped the repaired hearing aid in her ear. I could tell the minute she could hear us; Mom brightened up and *joined in the conversation. It was wonderful for her to be able to hear again, especially when all of us were laughing and marveling at the wonder we had just seen.*

Driving down that highway I remembered the prayers from that morning – those for faith and those for the hearing aid. I picked up a piece of the torn package and noticed that the address on the label had one number wrong. If Mom hadn't found the truck, the box would probably never have been delivered to our house. That thought sent another shiver up my spine in amazement at what I had just seen. I listened to the chatter in that car full of women who had just witnessed a miracle. Mom's and Dad's prayers had both been answered. She had her hearing aid, and we all grew a few notches that day.

SNAPSHOT 16

Conspiracy

I have an unusually strong bond with my daughter-in-law, Michelle. This is partly because our personalities compliment each other and partly because we have lived near each other and worked together for over 25 years. But mostly it's because she is such a wonderful person. Regardless of why, God brought a special bond between Michelle and me, and we are best friends.

Michelle's husband, Tim, can sometimes be a bit single-minded. This was never more evident than when he brought a beautiful Great Dane home and named it Clyde, after his father. A better name might have been "Collide." Michelle did her best to find the same joy in Clyde as Tim did, but she was having a difficult time being happy to have a pet the size of a Shetland pony living in her house. Clyde ate bags and bags of expensive dog food and then left equally large deposits in Michelle's back yard. His four large dusty feet left footprints all over her nice clean floors and worst of all, Clyde snacked on Michelle's leather boots, sandals and handbags.

"Tim," Michelle pleaded. "You have to do something about Clyde. He's too big for our little house, and he's ruining our home. I can't begin to keep things clean around here with him racing around everywhere with those big muddy feet."

"He's just a puppy," Tim said. "I'll work with him more and teach him some manners. He'll be okay."

Michelle wasn't convinced. She and I had more than one counseling session that was all about Clyde. Together we prayed that God would find a way to solve the Clyde problem.

But Clyde just kept growing, getting bigger and messier. It was even more challenging when Tim would play with Clyde in the house and the big dog would race around and around the house to Tim's cheers of encouragement.

"Tim!" Michelle begged as the dog raced around the coffee table and the centerpiece went crashing to the floor, "Make him stop!"

Tim kept clapping and encouraging Clyde to race around and around the house as furnishings flew and carpets rolled up. Michelle watched in horror as the dog's rowdiness exploded in her living room.

"Tim!" Michelle cried, but before she could get another word out, Clyde attempted to skid to a stop in front of their big picture window. When he couldn't stop in time, he crashed through the window and glass shattered all over the living room floor.

Michelle stood there vacillating between shock and anger.

Tim just laughed and got the broom.

Michelle left to find me. She showed up at our house in tears. "I don't know what to do, Mom," Michelle wiped away a tear that afternoon at my kitchen table. "I can't live with that dog anymore. And Tim cares more about Clyde than he does about me." She sobbed into her tissue.

I grabbed Michelle's hand and prayed that God would help Tim see how his love for the Great Dane was hurting his marriage. Michelle cried even harder, and it broke my heart to see this wonderful young woman so sad over my son's silly obsession with a dog.

"I've got an idea," I said to Michelle.

She stopped sniffling and looked up hopefully. "What kind of idea?"

"Go back home and tell Tim that he has to choose between you and the dog."

"He'll pick the dog," Michelle said sadly.

"Then you tell him you are leaving him and going to your mother's." I said firmly.

"Oh, he would be so embarrassed for my mom to think he cares more about his dog than about me," Michelle said wide eyed.

"You're right!" I agreed. "But you're not really going to go to your mother's. When you get to the state road, turn left and take the back roads to our house instead. I'm sure Tim will come here to try to figure out how to solve this. When he gets here I will give him a talking to."

"Do you think it will work?" Michelle asked hopefully.

"I'm sure once he sees how serious you are about him choosing you or Clyde, he'll be quick to fix this problem," I said confidently. I felt a little guilty setting up a plot like this with a little fib, but desperate times call for desperate measures.

Michelle went home and one more time begged Tim to find a new home for Clyde.

"Oh don't worry," Tim told Michelle. "That window thing was just a little accident. I'll make sure nothing like that ever happens again."

"So will I," Michelle said. "It's Clyde or me; take your pick. I'll be at my mom's house if you decide it's me you want and not that dog." She got in the car and locked all four doors as Tim tried to persuade her to stay. Determinedly, she drove away in the direction of her mother's home. When Michelle got to State highway she turned on a side road and drove directly to our house.

"I'm just so mad at him!" Michelle said, nervously wondering whether Tim would take her threat seriously.

"I am too," I told her.

Within minutes the phone rang. It was Tim.

"Mom, I've got a problem, and I need someone to talk to," Tim said.

"Come on over," I told him, feeling mildly ashamed that I had schemed with Michelle to get Tim to listen to reason.

Michelle and I danced around, laughing together, so happy that Tim was finally coming to his senses about this big unruly dog. Michelle had pulled her car around back so Tim couldn't see it when he drove up. When Tim came into the house he was extremely distressed.

"I've really messed up, Mom," he said shaking. "I can't believe she left, but I guess I should have listened to her."

"Yes," I said. "You should have. You need to make a choice. What are you going to do about it?"

Within minutes Tim had a plan that included a new window in the living room, a new home for Clyde and a wife who forgave him. Eventually Michelle and I confessed our plot to Tim, but Tim was so glad to have Michelle's forgiveness, he didn't mind. God has answered hundreds of prayers Michelle and I have prayed together over the years. But not one of those answered prayers stands out more vividly than our prayers together for a new home for Clyde.

SNAPSHOT 17

Grandpa's Homecoming Queen

I loved my Jewish family dearly and I have longed for them to know the joy and peace of the Lord. My daughter, Lori, was especially close to my father, and it was through Lori that I received one of the greatest blessings of my life.

Lori:

In the beginning of my junior year of high school, I attended a youth conference at Taylor University in Upland, Indiana, for prospective students. One of the conference group activities included writing down three prayer requests, putting the confidential list into a sealed envelope and writing my address on it. Our group leader promised to mail these envelopes to all of the students a year later. I had always longed for my Jewish family to hear and understand what the Bible said about Jesus, but knowing that there was a real "sensitivity" in the family about it, I had never spoken to my Grandpa about it. So the first thing I listed on my special prayer project was asking God to allow me an opportunity to talk to my Grandpa about Jesus and that Grandpa would be open and accepting of Jesus.

I accepted Christ as a young child and grew strong in my faith through the support and mentoring from Mom and Dad. I remember coming to a fork in the road right before entering Junior High. I knew that I had to make some choices. I either had to go with the crowd or take a stand. I took a stand. It wasn't a popular decision and consequently, I never really felt accepted by my peers in junior high and high school. I had developed a deep faith, and I lived it no matter what anyone else at school thought. It did get a bit lonely and difficult at times. God spared me from experimenting in the risky ways my peers did, and I was often teased about my clean lifestyle when classmates would come in on Mondays after their wild weekends.

I really didn't feel like I was missing out on too much because there was always so much fun activity going on at home and at the church. But nevertheless, many times the unkind words and actions hurt deep inside. Mom and Dad prayed and coached me through it and continually shared scripture with me.

My first few years of high school were challenging for me. I didn't feel accepted. It wasn't cool to be a dedicated Christian, but as I became an upper classman, things started to change. I noticed a different level of respect and kindness from many of my peers. By the end of my junior year, after several recommendations from staff and students, I was elected president of the student council. I knew that I wasn't elected because of popularity, but I did sense a new level of respect – something I had not experienced before in these circles. The following year I was very shocked and surprised when I was nominated along with several other girls for Homecoming queen.

I had always thought that Homecoming court was a popularity contest. How could this be? I never dreamed in a million years that I would even be on the radar. Other classmates felt the same way I did and before long I came to understand how complicated a trivial high school social title could become.

The first inkling that something was amiss happened when my favorite teacher, Mr. Herald called me out of class.

"Lori," Mr. Herald looked grim. "I just want you to know that there is a petition being circulated about you."

"Me?" I gasped. "Why?"

"Well," Mr. Herald took off his glasses and nervously rubbed a spot between his eyes, "I know it's nothing. But they want to *impeach you from your position as president on student council."*

"Why? What did I do?" I asked in shock. There hadn't been any conflicts on the council brought to my attention. Our group had been working very smoothly.

"You didn't do anything," Mr. Herald said. "There is no validity to the petition claims. I think this is more about diverting attention from your nomination for Homecoming queen. But don't let it get to you girl. Be strong; be brave."

I was stunned, and I wanted to cry. Just when I thought things had turned around I found myself to be a target. I fought back the tears and expressed how thankful I was that Mr. Herald took the time to tell me. The bell rang for school to be dismissed, and students began pouring out of the classrooms. I nodded another whispered thank you to Mr. Herald and ran to catch the bus for home. If I could just keep my emotions together until I got home, I knew I would be okay. Mom would be there, and that's who I really needed to comfort and counsel me.

I got on the bus and sat down by a window and looked out through blurry eyes. Over and over in my head I just prayed to make it home without falling apart. The seven miles to our house seemed like 70, but I didn't cry until I stepped off the bus. As soon as my foot hit the ground, I burst into tears, and I was sobbing by the time I ran through the door.

I was relieved that Mom was there, and she was wonderful. She cried with me and we prayed together, asking God to give me strength to face the situation and to forgive those who had been so vengeful. Dad came right over from the church office where he was studying, next door. He too prayed for me and gave me a pep talk, coaching me into holding my head high and realizing that no matter how things turned out, I was a child of the King of Kings.

I gathered my courage and went to school the next day, holding my head high and praying with every step I took. My pain actually turned into a super-natural adrenalin rush. God gave me the strength to smile and nod to everyone as if nothing was wrong. I wasn't sure who was behind the scenes causing all this trouble, but it didn't matter. Mom's and Dad's words played like a tape recorder in my head, "Lori, you are a child of the King of Kings."

When I got to my locker, someone had posted hate mail on the door. It was frightening, but I gently took it down and prayed that God would help me to grasp all that Mom and Dad had shared with me. I remembered those Bible verses that brought strength and comfort.

Back then, churches discouraged teens from going to dances. I had never attended a school dance. I was surprised when the dean of students called me to his office.

"Lori," he began, as I braced myself, "I know your stand on dancing and that you don't participate in any of our school dances. But what are you going to do about Homecoming? What if you are elected Homecoming Queen? The Homecoming queen has always attended the dance; it's a ball held in the queen's honor."

I didn't even pause to think about it. "Well, I don't go to dances," I told him, shrugging my shoulders. "So if I am required to go to the dance to be Homecoming queen, then I guess it would be best to be removed from the list of nominees."

The dean looked at me thoughtfully and said, "Well Lori, I guess if the student body elects you as their Homecoming queen, knowing where you stand, then they must really want you to be their queen. I don't want to stand in their way. It will be the first time in the history of Quincy High School that the Queen will not be at her own ball."

I felt blessed by his perspective.

The students voted for Homecoming queen at school the day of the Homecoming football game. I was surprised that day when I was called to the office just before second period with a note to call home. The note said "urgent."

Nervously I dialed home and waited for Mom to answer. After two rings, I didn't even say who was calling; Mom just spoke right up, "Lori, you are going to win. I just know it."

"Mom, shhhhh, please!" I was hoping nobody could hear her excitement over the phone in the office. "I need to get back to class. I have an English vocabulary quiz to take," I told her.

"You're not listening," Mom persisted. "I was reading my morning devotions today. It was Second Timothy, in chapter four. Listen to this..." Mom took a deep breath. "I have fought the good fight, I have finished the race, I have kept the faith. Now there is in store for me the crown of righteousness, which the Lord, the righteous Judge, will award to me on that day."

"You think that scripture means I'm going to win?" I whispered doubtfully.

"God put it there for me to read today," Mom said. "The crown! Oh Lori, I think we should have a party to celebrate. I'm going to start planning right now."

I went back to class in wonder, and hope started to stir in me ever so slightly; but the reality of the situation kept me from dreaming too big. I tried to stay focused on the usual routine of Friday exams. Win or lose, I still needed to pass my classes.

Through all the flurry of Homecoming distraction, Dad was a rock. He sat down with me and encouraged me with fatherly wisdom.

"Lori," Dad said. "It's such an honor for you to be nominated for Homecoming queen, and you have handled all of this commotion very well. You've made me so proud."

Dad shifted in his chair as I gulped and nodded a silent thank you. Then Dad continued, "Now, you do know that the chances of getting elected, as the queen are pretty slim, right? I mean, our lifestyle isn't too popular. Just go to that game tonight with your head held high, knowing that you have honored God with your decisions about your life. So, Baby, try not to be too disappointed if you don't win, okay?"

I hugged him in agreement and then Dad sang to me, the way he had so many times since I was a toddler, "There she is — Miss America!" If nothing else happened tonight, at least I knew that I was loved and adored by my father.

The name of the Homecoming queen would be announced at the Friday night football game. The nominees were introduced in front of the crowd at halftime and all the girls' fathers were the escorts. I had chosen a floor length, mint green empire style formal with a swishy skirt, topped with a bolero jacket, accented with a pair of sparkly silver heels. Mom loaned me an elegant glittery necklace and bracelet and walking with my arm in Dad's, I felt like a real princess.

My grandma and grandpa came all the way from Kalamazoo, not to watch the game, but to see the halftime pageantry. It was chilly under the football lights in the Michigan autumn night. I was nervous and excited to be part of the group, despite all the grief I'd been through. Unlike Mom, I didn't expect to win. I was sure another girl who was very popular with all the boys would take the title, but I was thoroughly enjoying the night and all of the hubbub.

After the girls and their fathers drove up in convertibles, we were lined up in the middle of the football field. The announcer called out over the loudspeaker, "And the 1976 Homecoming Queen is ..." The name was muffled, and I didn't hear it.

The crowd started clapping, and I didn't know who they were cheering for, so I looked down the row of girls to see the winner's reaction.

Dad leaned down to whisper in my ear, "I think they said your name, Baby."

A little embarrassed, I said, "No Daddy. I don't think so."

I looked again at the girls to see who it was, and they were all looking at me.

The announcer repeated it again, "The 1976 Homecoming queen is Lori Mills."

This time I heard it. I couldn't believe it! I was in shock. I looked up at my Dad, and his eyes were filled with tears.

He said, "Congratulations Baby. Congratulations."

I looked up into the bleachers where my family and friends were sitting. There was my little Jewish grandpa, dressed all in black, standing up and waving his beret back and forth with his arm extended over his head. He was shouting, "That's my granddaughter! That's my granddaughter!" It was truly my own "Fiddler-on-the-Roof" moment.

They placed a tiara on my head and a ribbon sash over my shoulder and the celebration music played. All of the girls on the court were very gracious and each gave me a big hug. Then Dad escorted me into the back of a new convertible sports car for a lap around the football field.

I waved to the crowd with a big smile, and a full heart. As the car turned the second corner, Dad handed me a small gift box. It was a charm that said '1976 Homecoming Queen.'

"How did you know?" I gasped.

Dad laughed, "I didn't, but your Mom insisted that I have it in my pocket because she just knew it was going to happen."

When we came to the last corner of the victory lap, several of the students who had tried to impeach me from student council revealed themselves by the obscenities that they were yelling. But their loud voices were drowned out very quickly not only by the crowd cheering and the joy of the moment, but also by that wonderful tape recorder in my head, with Mom and Dad's voices and challenges, that carried me through those difficult days that led up to this amazing experience.

As promised, Mom had arranged a big party at our house, and friends and family turned out to celebrate. Usually everyone gathered in our large family room in the lower level of our house. But tonight for some reason, everyone was upstairs in the kitchen; everyone but Grandpa. After I had greeted everyone, I missed Grandpa, and I went to look for him. I found him downstairs in the family room all by himself.

Running down the stairs, I called out, "Grandpa? Are you down here? What are you doing down here all alone?"

"Oh Lori," Grandpa patted the arm of the big chair where he was sitting, and I sat down there next to him. "I was just thinking about you. I am just so proud of you. I can't even express how much pride I feel for you right now."

I smiled at him and gave him a big hug. "Thank you, Grandpa. I'm so glad you came tonight."

"Me too," Grandpa hugged me back. "I am just so proud to be your Grandpa."

"Grandpa," I pulled back and looked him directly in the eye. "I have to tell you that what you are proud of is really not me. It's Jesus in me. I didn't win because I'm special or popular. I won because the kids at school really respect my walk with Jesus. It's not because of me, but because of Him. "

Grandpa listened intently and nodded. Tears filled his eyes.

I pushed myself up straighter on the arm of the chair and continued, "Grandpa, I know that you are Jewish and that you've been taught that Jesus is not the Messiah. But Jesus said in the Bible, I am the way the truth and the life." Tears began to fill my eyes as I talked. "And he goes on to say, no man comes to the Father, but by me."

A tear rolled down Grandpa's cheek. I put my hand on his and said, "The Bible says that if we don't have Jesus in our hearts, we won't be in heaven. Grandpa, I just can't imagine being in heaven without you."

Grandpa nodded. It was such a sweet exchange and very emotional. I choked up in my tears, and I stepped out of the room to get a tissue. Just then my oldest brother, Mike came down the stairs. He noticed my hasty exit and asked Grandpa, "What's wrong with Lori?"

"Lori has too much love in her heart," Grandpa said wiping his eyes. "That's what's wrong with Lori."

The next day when Mike revealed his conversation with Grandpa, I realized that my sweet Jewish grandfather knew that my brief chat with him about Jesus was in love and not for any other reason. It warmed my heart to know that Grandpa was so tender about it.

About a month later, I received that letter from Taylor University, addressed to me in my own handwriting. It was the prayer request list that I had prayed about the year before and had completely forgotten about it. What a joy to realize that God answered the first prayer request on the list – that I would be able to share my faith with my grandfather.

Several years later, when I received the news that my Grandpa had died, I was heartbroken. But I was also relieved that I had seized the opportunity to share Jesus with him and *that Grandpa had responded so beautifully. Shortly after the funeral, my grandmother gave Mom a cherished treasure from Grandpa's wallet. It was a photo of my mother, which he had wrapped in this poem. As sad as it was to lose this kind, gentle man from my life, his message to us through leaving this poem with my mother's photo will forever be cherished:*

> I counted dollars, while God counted crosses;
> I counted gains, while God counted losses.
> I counted my worth, my things gained in store;
> And He sized me up by the scars that I bore.
> I counted honors and sought degrees,
> He counted the hours I spent on my knees.
> I never knew until one day by the grave
> How vain are the things that we spend life to save.

Clyde:

For years, Gerrie's father told both Gerrie and me that he enjoyed listening to the Billy Graham Crusades on television whenever Gerrie's mother wasn't present. We will not be surprised to see Grandpa in Heaven when our family is all reunited with Jesus one day.

SNAPSHOT 18

Miracle In A Concert Hall

A number of years back, Clyde accepted a job as a pastor at a church in Naples, Florida. When I arrived in Naples, I decided it was the most beautiful city in the world. And over the next ten years, I concluded that I was right. Naples is an amazing place to call home. What more can a girl ask for than to have one of the most beautiful beaches in the world just 15 minutes from home? Naples is an upscale community, filled with art galleries, shopping centers, golf courses and that magnificent beach on the Gulf of Mexico. Clyde was a senior pastor, on a tight budget, and everyone but Clyde and his secretary were volunteers.

Our church worship services were led with piano and organ music. Our piano player was a willing volunteer who had reached age 80. Her heart was in the right place, but in her advanced years, her fingers didn't cooperate on the keys very well. She wanted to retire and asked us to find a replacement, but she agreed to stay on until we filled the position.

Clyde and I, and many of our members, had asked around looking for a pianist, but we hadn't found anyone even remotely interested. With our tight budget, we were looking for a volunteer – someone who would donate their talents to our church, so there was no point in advertising the position. It was complicated because hiring a pianist is a delicate issue for a church. The pianist plays an integral part of worship. An applicant for a pianist has to be more than just a musician; he or she has to have the right musical style, strong leadership qualities and be a good fit spiritually.

Over and over we prayed, "Lord you know that we need a pianist for worship. Please put the right person in our midst."

A long time went by – it seemed like a very long time - and no one ever inquired about playing the piano for our church. As our aging pianist in residence continued to help us out, her skills deteriorated even more. Clyde and I kept praying, asking God to send us a musician to enrich our Sunday services.

There was a Gaither Concert being held about 50 miles from home, and Clyde and I planned to attend with a group from our church. It was a good thing that we bought our tickets early, because it was a sold-out house, and the place was packed when we arrived. We found seats, and I lead our group into a long row and sat down just as the music began.

At intermission the woman seated next to me, left briefly and returned with a Gaither piano book that she put down in the space between us. It had a big photo of Gloria Gaither on the cover, and that caught my eye.

"Oh, I just love her," I said, as I picked up the book and affectionately brushed my hand over the cover. "Doesn't she just look beautiful?" I asked the book's owner. I opened the book and began to thumb through the pages, when I noticed the musical scores inside.

"Oh, I didn't buy it for the picture," the woman replied. "I bought it to play the piano. I just love the Gaithers' music."

"Oh! You play piano?" I gasped, wondering if piano and Gaither had some significance for me.

"Yes," the woman said, "That is, I used to play, but I've been away from it for awhile. My name is Beverly," she extended her hand.

"Hello, Beverly," I replied and shook her hand. "We have been looking for a piano player for our church," I broached the subject carefully. "In fact, we've been looking for what seems like forever. We haven't been able to find anyone in Naples that will fit in to our style of worship."

"Is your church in Naples?" Beverly asked quizzically. "I live in Naples."

The music started about then, but I could barely sit still to listen. I had just found a pianist who lived in Naples, who liked Gaither music, and she was sitting right next to me! I tried to whisper this bit of news to Clyde who shushed me and kept listening to the Gaithers. Didn't he realize that I had something to tell him that was far more important than the song he had heard a million times?

After the concert, I finally got to introduce Beverly to Clyde, and he invited her to drop by the church to audition. He gave Beverly his business card.

Beverly said. "I'll come by and play one day soon." She took Clyde's card and laughed. "Oh my!" Beverly said with a twinkle in her eye. "Is this the street address for the church?"

Clyde nodded.

Beverly's smile broadened. "It's just a mile or so up the street from my house." Beverly gathered her things and left the concert waving good bye.

I was disappointed. "Why didn't you hire her right now?" I asked Clyde, tugging at his elbow.

"I don't know if she can play!" Clyde defended his decision. "She might play with just one finger. I want to hear her music before I just invite her to play for worship." I knew he was right, but I wanted a pianist so badly, and I just knew in my heart that this was God's perfect timing. Today God had put this woman right next to me in that concert hall. There was no doubt in my heart.

About a week later, Beverly came by and auditioned beautifully for Clyde, and she was hired. Not only could she play for our worship style, but Beverly also played in a very similar style as Clyde's mother. God had finally sent us the proper person to meet our needs. As Beverly's talent emerged, our membership grew and more and more musically talented people began to surface. Beverly developed friendships easily and soon she had a whole church family, along with Clyde and me, who loved her and appreciated her many gifts.

Clyde and I discovered that Beverly had been hurt in a previous church and had not found a church home in Naples. She had become discouraged and disenchanted with church membership. But the opportunity to be our pianist beckoned, and Beverly was perfect for the job. As a daughter of a pastor, Beverly had years of experience as a church pianist and knew how to step into the role. Clyde and I encouraged Beverly as a worship team leader, and soon she was switching from piano to organ, serving as both pianist and choir director. Her musical talents were maximized through the church, and Beverly began to heal from her prior church experience. As our prayers for a pianist were answered, Beverly's prayers were as well. God had provided a good fit for both Beverly and also for our church. For, as Beverly met our needs for a pianist and organist, the musical opportunities and spiritual growth of being in this worship team leader position far exceeded Beverly's prayers.

I often reflect on how I met Beverly that day at the Gaither concert. I stumbled onto a qualified, trained, experienced church pianist at a concert 50 miles from home. Out of all the people sitting in that sold-out auditorium, I sat down next to a pianist who lived just down the street. I believe God had his hand on that. He had answered my prayer for a pianist, just when I needed one the most.

SNAPSHOT 19

Marlene And The Red Eye Flight That Changed Her Life

My oldest son, Mike, was a national Christian youth speaker and traveled all over the country for speaking engagements. One night at the end of a speaking tour, Mike was on a red-eye flight out of Dallas, headed to San Diego where his brother Andy lived. As a seasoned business traveler, Mike elected to sit in the back of the plane, with a handful of passengers spaced far apart, where he could relax and catch some sleep.

A very attractive flight attendant brought him a soft drink and noticed the logo stitched on his jacket. It read "The Rock."

"What does that represent?" she asked Mike.

"It's the theme for a speaking tour I'm on. Jesus is the Rock." Mike told her.

"What line of work are you in?" the flight attendant asked.

"I'm a national Christian youth speaker," Mike explained. "I just finished a speaking engagement, and now before I head home to my wife, I'm going to visit my brother."

The flight attendant extended her hand in greeting, "I'm Marlene," she said. "When I get a break, I'd like to talk to you." She smiled weakly and moved on down the aisle of the plane to attend to the other passengers.

Mike opened his book, and relaxed as the flight continued on toward San Diego. About a half hour later, Marlene returned and sat down in the seat next to him.

"Okay," Marlene said taking a deep breath, "I have some questions."

"I'll do my best to answer them," Mike said and closed his book.

Marlene pushed a strand of long blonde hair behind her ear as she began to explain the challenges in her life. Despite the appearance of perfection, Marlene was very unhappy in her personal and professional life. She told Mike about the numerous places she traveled and the various service awards she had received, including one for preventing a hijacking by talking someone out of using a gun. Yet the glamour of being a flight attendant had faded, and Marlene felt restless when she flew.

Personally, Marlene was a beautiful woman. But Mike noticed that Marlene lacked sparkle. As she explained to Mike that she enjoyed a comfortable lifestyle with a successful husband in San Diego, Marlene's eyes clouded when she mentioned her husband. While financially successful, Marlene's husband was abusive and unfaithful.

"Everything is unraveling in my life," Marlene said tearfully. "My marriage is falling apart. I'm so unhappy in my career, and my life has no meaning. I feel so empty, and I don't know what to do about it. Tonight, right here on this plane, during take off, I tightened my seatbelt and cried to God for help."

"Obviously, God heard your prayers," Mike said confidently.

"What do you mean?" Marlene asked curiously.

"He sent somebody on this flight who could help." Mike said. "Marlene, Jesus Christ can fill those parts of your life where you feel empty."

Marlene looked at Mike doubtfully, but she continued to listen.

Mike continued, "Marlene, in every crisis, Jesus is the answer. If you're interested, I can explain how He can help you and how Jesus can change your life."

Marlene's eyes brightened, and she said, "I am."

Since the plane was nearly empty, and all the passengers were settled down, Mike was able to have a lengthy discussion with Marlene as he explained the Gospel and that God had a plan for her life. He wrote down four spiritual laws on a cocktail napkin as he outlined how God could become the focal point for her life.

God loves you and has a plan for your life.

Man is sinful and separated from God. He cannot know and experience God's love and plan for his life.

Jesus Christ is God's only provision for man's sin. Through Him, you can know and experience God's love and plan for your life.

We must individually receive Jesus Christ as Savior and Lord; then we can know and experience God's love and plan for our lives.

Marlene had many questions for Mike, and he tried his best to answer each one. As the plane began to descend into San Diego, Marlene thanked Mike for talking with her.

"If you're interested to know more," Mike told Marlene, "My brother, Andy, attends a great church in San Diego. He and his wife Cathy hold a Bible study at their home, and I know you would be welcome to attend." Mike wrote down Andy's address and phone number and gave it to Marlene.

Marlene smiled as she read the address. "This is very near my home," she said as she folded the paper and tucked it into her pocket.

A few days later Marlene pulled up in a beautiful Mercedes Benz at Andy's house, just before their weekly Bible study. She met Andy and Cathy who welcomed her into their home, gave her a Bible and invited her to church.

About a month later, Clyde and I went to visit Andy and Cathy. We went to worship services on Sunday, and as Clyde and I were entering the church of about 3,000 worshippers, an attractive woman came up behind us.

"I'll bet you're Andy's parents," she said. "I'm Marlene, and I've heard so much about both of you," Marlene said as she introduced herself.

"How did she know we were Andy's parents? We've never been to this church before." I wondered to myself. I looked at Marlene quizzically. She was dressed in a cream-colored dress that sort of floated about her slender body. She looked like an angel. Clyde and I invited her to sit with us.

As we waited for the service to begin, Marlene chatted and explained how she had come to enjoy the Bible study at Andy and Cathy's house. This was her first Sunday at this big church and she was looking forward to making new friends here.

After the service, Clyde and Marlene began a conversation while I went to look for Andy and Cathy.

Clyde asked Marlene if she had ever asked Jesus to come into her heart.

"No," Marlene said sadly. "I haven't."

As everyone exited that large church, two people remained – Marlene and Clyde. And on her knees, Marlene asked Jesus to come into her heart and life.

That evening, I wasn't feeling well, but Clyde and Andy returned to the church for evening worship. Marlene joined them at the church. A former Hell's Angel gave his testimony at that service, and Marlene was impressed with the promise of how God could turn lives around. The young flight attendant was excited to begin to face her life with God as her co-pilot.

The next day when I was feeling better, I asked Andy how to reach Marlene. I wanted to talk with her and encourage her in her new walk with God.

"How can I call her?" I asked Andy. "I want to meet her for coffee."

"I don't know, Mom." Andy said. "She didn't give me her phone number."

"Well she comes to your Bible study. You must have some record of Marlene," I persisted.

"Honestly, I don't know, Mom." Andy said. "Marlene just showed up that first night, and she's been coming ever since. She came to worship for the first time last Sunday, but beyond that, Cathy and I don't know much about her."

"Well, I want to see her before we go home," I said determinedly. "I'm going to pray."

But San Diego is a big city of over three million people. There was no telephone listing for Marlene, and no one had any idea how to reach her. But I couldn't let it go. I was determined to find Marlene before we headed back to Chicago.

That day, as we headed out for some sight-seeing and shopping, I looked at gas stations, convenience stores, dress shops, restaurants, auto repair places, in doorways; everywhere we went I kept searching, hoping to find Marlene. As we drove back to Andy's house, I looked down every drive way, across every intersection and anywhere I thought I might find Marlene, praying continuously that I could find her. I felt so confident that I would bump into her, but I didn't.

Despite being discouraged, I continued to pray that I would find Marlene before we left San Diego. She had to be somewhere in there among those three million people!

The next day Clyde and I went to the airport to head back to Chicago. We made our way to the waiting area at the gate, and Clyde sat down to read the newspaper. But I didn't want to sit. I wanted to check on our seating, and then I went window shopping at the little stores and kiosks. All the while I was still thinking about finding Marlene. It just didn't feel right, leaving San Diego without seeing her. I was looking at San Diego key chains hanging on a gift shop display when an employee door far across the hallway opened. I looked up and who walked out of that door, but a smartly-styled flight attendant named Marlene. Our eyes met, and when Marlene recognized me, she screamed, and I screamed, and we had a joyful celebration in the airport gift shop.

"Marlene, I've been praying that I would find you before I went home," I said, holding her hand. "And here you are!" I started tugging her down the hallway toward the gate where Clyde was waiting.

Marlene laughed and ran with me cheerfully. "I'm not even supposed to be here," she said. "It's my day off. But the girl who was supposed to work today called in sick."

"Well, I'm so glad to see you," I told her. "I just didn't want to leave San Diego without having a chance to talk to you again."

"Well, I have about 20 minutes. Let's chat," Marlene said. "Where are you flying today?" she asked.

Before I answered, I felt that familiar shiver of God's presence. "Clyde and I are flying to Chicago." I pulled out my boarding pass to check the departure time. "We leave in about an hour," I told her.

"I'm working that flight!" Marlene said joyfully.

Clyde and I enjoyed chatting with Marlene throughout the flight home, and this time I exchanged contact information with her. We invited Marlene to visit us, and when she came to see us we were planning one of our trips to Israel.

"Oh, I want to go!" Marlene exclaimed. So we took her with us to visit the Holy Land and while we were there, Clyde baptized Marlene in the Jordan River. As God worked in

Marlene's life, her outlook on life improved, and she became happy and content with the many ways God had blessed her. Eventually Marlene remarried and enjoyed a happy, successful marriage.

It's been years now, but Clyde and I keep in contact with Marlene. Both Mike and Andy enjoy hearing updates on her life. Marlene is a steadfast believer who thanks God for answering her desperate prayer back on that red-eye flight from Dallas with a few words written on a cocktail napkin.

SNAPSHOT 20

Keys In The Ocean

In my first book, *Oy Vey! Such a Deal*, I told a true story of finding our lost keys at the bottom of the ocean. It received so many comments from readers that I would like to tell it again.

Our children were all grown and on their own when Clyde took a job as a pastor in Naples, Florida. Naples is on the gulf side of Florida and it has the most beautiful beach I've ever seen. Most days, no matter what the weather, Clyde and I would drive to a beach parking lot, and then walk about two miles up the beach, turn around and walk back. The beach was beautiful, with white sand, aqua blue water and bordered by a gated community made up of million dollar homes. Clyde and I loved these moments on the beach, often walking hand in hand, and I was constantly thanking God for blessing us with this beach.

One summer morning, Clyde and I parked the car and made our way up the beach. There wasn't much wind, and the sun was hot. Before long, Clyde handed me his shirt and went out into the surf to cool off. The water was shallow, and Clyde had to walk about 80 yards out before he could actually swim. I stood on the shore, watching my tanned husband as he played in the water. He was enjoying the surf, cooling off and diving in and out of the water like a dolphin.

I watched Clyde awhile, and then I decided to walk a bit farther up the beach, kicking the water with my feet to stay cool. The seagulls were soaring overhead, and I could see boats out on the calm water. I took a deep breath and for about the millionth time, I thanked God that I was blessed to live in Naples near this beautiful beach.

Suddenly, Clyde jogged up behind me, and he had a funny look on his face. I stopped to let him catch his breath. I knew something was up, but he didn't look ill or injured, so I wasn't concerned. "What's wrong?" I asked.

"Ahm.... I don't think I have the keys," Clyde said.

The keys. He meant the key ring filled with keys for everything: the house, the cars, the church, the mailbox, the church mailbox... they were all on that key ring. He couldn't have lost them.

"Check your pockets," I said instantly.

Clyde checked every pocket, but he didn't find our keys.

"Did you leave them in the car?" I asked. I checked the pockets in my swimsuit cover-up, even though I was certain that I had never been in possession of our keys.

"No, I had them when I took my shirt off," Clyde said. "I didn't want to leave them on the beach by my towel when I went in the water. I was afraid someone might steal them. I put them in my swimsuit pocket."

"Well, check your shorts pocket!" I said, getting frustrated that he could be so irresponsible.

"I did," Clyde said with a small smile. "But the keys are not in my shorts pockets. I checked all four of the pockets several times. The keys are gone."

Clyde was grinning like a little boy, but I was beginning to panic in my frustration. How could he be so careless to put the car keys in his pocket and then go swimming?

"Well, we have to find them," I said to Clyde, and I turned around and headed back the way he had come from.

We walked back toward the area where we thought Clyde had been swimming, but the tide was coming in, erasing all signs of where we had stood just a few minutes earlier. "You start looking, and I'll start praying," I ordered Clyde.

Clyde walked straight out into the surf until the water was chest-high. It was about the same distance he had walked earlier. Then he turned left and began to walk slowly, feeling the bottom of the ocean with his toes. The gulf coast water was frothy and Clyde couldn't see the sand below him. So he just dragged his toes in front of him, and then felt the ocean floor with his feet, hoping to feel the keys. He walked and turned, walked and turned, slowly using his feet trying to find the keys. Up and down, up and down, Clyde kept going under and surfacing, like a dolphin.

I was on the beach, pacing and praying. "Lord, you are the only one who knows where those keys are," I cried. "Please help Clyde to find them. We need those keys Lord. It's not just the car keys! The keys to our life are on that ring!"

I kept pacing and praying, waving my hands around, dragging my fingers through my hair. I knew I was a sight, but I didn't care if anyone else saw me, I just kept praying. "Please help us find those keys, Lord. We need the keys for the car and our house and the church and the mail box! Please help Clyde to find them. I promise that if you help Clyde find those keys, I will spend the rest of my life telling the world You did it."

I paused and looked out into the ocean where Clyde continued to walk a bit, easing his way across the ocean floor, trying to find the keys with his toes. I thought about going for help, but I didn't think I would even be able to get into the gated community of million dollar homes to knock on a door. And what kind of help would I ask for? I couldn't just walk up to a mansion, knock on the door and ask to use their phone.

I kept praying, and Clyde kept searching among the sand and surf. He was into a rhythm now, taking a step, pausing, and then walking another step. I held my hand up to shade my eyes as I watched him from shore, as over and over, Clyde would walk a step and pause, walk a step and pause, making a slow and deliberate search below the gray, murky water.

I vacillated from pleading with God to holding my breath as I looked out into the surf when suddenly Clyde stopped. I couldn't see what was happening, just that Clyde was bending over. And then I screamed for joy when Clyde held up the keys high in the air.

I have told this story to thousands and thousands of people over the years through my speaking engagements, tours and in *Oy Vey! Such a Deal.* It was a moment of faith that I will never forget.

That miracle spoke to me loud and clear that God wants us to be faithful and to take our problems to Him. Whether it's the lost car keys, the children's health, an empty refrigerator or the light bill, God wants us to trust Him for all of our needs. He has it in his control – all things are in His control, even locating a small key ring at the bottom of the ocean.

SNAPSHOT 21

Mirror, Mirror On The Wall

I was in high school in the 1950's, and it was customary for my Jewish girlfriends to have plastic surgery to reshape their noses on their 16th birthdays. It was common in our Jewish community when you turned 16. I started dreaming about having my nose "done" in my pre-teen years, but as my 16th birthday neared, I was dismayed when my father, who usually granted me my every wish, said no.

It wasn't as if my nose was huge, but childhood insecurities have a way of hanging around long after we leave childhood behind. My mother was always correcting me, adjusting me or pointing out ways she thought I could improve my looks. I was confident on many levels as I entered adulthood, but I always longed for the plastic surgery that would give me that "Debbie Reynolds" nose. After I was married, a family friend offered to do my nose for free. Clyde and my father both insisted that I looked beautiful the way God made me, and so I had to decline the generous offer. I was so mad though that I jumped in our green Ford and sped away on two wheels around every corner.

As I approached my senior years, I began observing my aging process, and I didn't like it. I love fashion, accessorizing, and I enjoy looking my best. But as I grew older, it became more and more difficult to feel that I had achieved my "best" in my physical appearance. I try to take good care of myself physically by exercising, eating right and avoiding harmful habits. But despite all that I've done to care for myself, gravity was not my friend as I entered my 70's.

One day, a few weeks before my 70th birthday, a friend asked me to go with her to a lecture by Dr. Jasper, a local plastic surgeon. I tagged along with her, and as I sat in the meeting room, I was intrigued by Dr. Jasper's kind manner and the care and concern he seemed to have for his patients. The longer the distinguished, tanned surgeon talked, the more interested I became. As Dr. Jasper wrapped up his presentation I felt that deep down desire from my youth re-emerge with a voice that said, "Gerrie, he could make you look better."

I sat there for awhile as the other women chatted and began to leave. I thought about how many times I sat in front of my mirror, pulling my loose skin up from under my chin, back toward my ears to see how much better I'd look if I had plastic surgery to tuck it all back.

I was fascinated by what I had just heard. Dr. Jasper's technique didn't seem to be all that invasive; in fact, it was out-patient surgery. The doctor was fully licensed, seemed extremely competent and would do the surgery at a surgical center. Patients who had this surgery went home right out of the recovery room. It took a few days for the scars to heal, but that part didn't frighten me. The more information I gathered from Dr. Jasper, the more interested I became. And then, what started out as an appealing idea became a deep desire.

During refreshments, Dr. Jasper and I were chatting. First we talked about our hobbies, and I learned that he was so tan from gardening. Dr. Jasper was an avid gardener, and he told me a little about his flowers. But then I steered the conversation back toward me. Actually, I drove it all about me, asking him a lot of questions specific to my looks.

"Just make an appointment," Dr. Jasper said in his kind, professional manner. "We can talk about what your goals are, and I can recommend some procedures."

"Well, I just have a few more questions," I said, not ready to commit to an office visit. I didn't know what Clyde would say, and on a pastor's salary we certainly didn't have the money for such a luxury.

"And I would love to answer them," Dr. Jasper said with a smile. "Here's my card. Call my office, and schedule an appointment. It's a free consultation."

I called Dr. Jasper's office the next day, and the receptionist scheduled an appointment for the end of the month. That gave me plenty of time to pray. I started thinking how wonderful it would be to not have all these wrinkles that made me look much older than I felt. The desire grew a bit more in my heart for the plastic surgery but then I'd have a flash of guilt, and I'd wonder, is this desire just for my vanity? Yes, I admitted to myself it was; I didn't like looking old. I wanted to look my best, just as I had lived all my life. And that desire for the surgery was right back in the forefront of my thoughts.

I didn't tell Clyde. I talked and laughed about it with my friend, but it was just all in fun. There was no way I could afford a facelift like a lot of my friends were having. The cost was $15,000 to $25,000 depending on what was done. My medical health insurance plan wouldn't cover this kind of expense, yet I continued to daydream of how wonderful it would be to have Dr. Jasper perform his magic on me.

Vainly I told the Lord, "It would be so wonderful. But Lord, do I even dare ask you such a thing?"

The desire just loomed larger each day as my appointment approached. I continued to pray, "Lord I know it's not necessary, but it would be good for my confidence and my ability to continue to speak in front of others in my older years. I know a facelift isn't a vital surgery, but it would be a great boost of encouragement for me."

The desire continued to grow within me to have a facelift, so I went for the free consultation. Right away I felt camaraderie with Dr. Jasper as he explained what he would do and what results I could expect. He was thoughtful as he evaluated my needs and confident in his recommendations. Dr. Jasper was tender to my desire for a facelift, but when he told me how much it would cost, I was startled. I had no idea that it would cost so much! I thanked him for his time but explained that the cost would surely prohibit me from having the procedures he described.

"Well, Gerrie," Dr. Jasper asked, "How much can you afford to pay?"

Guiltily, I looked at this kind surgeon and admitted, "Nothing."

"Nothing?" Dr. Jasper asked.

"No," I said guiltily, "My husband is a pastor, and we can't afford this." I gestured around the room. "You have been so kind to meet with me, but I'm afraid that I have taken up your time needlessly."

"I see," Dr. Jasper said, making some notes on my chart.

"You see, Dr. Jasper," I started to confess. "All my life I have wanted to have plastic surgery. I had just about given up on the idea, when my friend invited me to your presentation. I've been praying and praying that God would find a way for me to have you do my facelift. But I really don't have the money, and I shouldn't have even made the appointment."

Dr. Jasper looked thoughtful for a moment. He was the most respected and esteemed plastic surgeon in the Sacramento Region, and I was so embarrassed for taking up his time. I sat there, staring at the floor and wishing there was a trap door right there so I could escape, when to my surprise Dr. Jasper put his pen in his pocket and offered his services as a gift to me. I would still have to pay for the surgical room costs, and a few other incidentals, but most of the costs would be a gift from this generous surgeon.

I could hardly wait to get home to tell Clyde. I had just received the biggest of my heart's desires! I was going to have a facelift, and I could hardly wait.

But when I got home, Clyde thought I was absolutely crazy. "You don't need a facelift!" Clyde exclaimed. "I love you just the way you are."

"What?" I said, "With this saggy neck?" And I grabbed the loose skin beneath my chin.

Yes," Clyde said. "Saggy neck and all. And besides," Clyde continued logically. "What well-known plastic surgeon would be willing to do this kind of expensive procedure for the cost of the surgery room?"

"My dear Dr. Jasper, that's who," I told Clyde. "I've been praying about this for over a week, and God has answered my prayer."

I continued to pray as my surgery date approached. As much as I prayed about my surgery, I also prayed that my friends would follow me as a referral, to repay this gallant doctor.

Clyde had no idea that this was major surgery. I didn't really know how to describe the procedure or what to expect in recovery. I thought it would be just a nip and a tuck, plus a couple of stitches. So, since Clyde had a softball game that morning, he dropped me off and asked our daughter Lori to pick me up.

I wasn't deceiving Clyde about my surgery. I didn't really know what to expect. I was so excited when Dr. Jasper had offered to do my surgery as a gift; the rest of the information just sort of flew out of my head. Clyde dropped me off at the surgery center, and the nurse told him to be back in about five hours.

"Our daughter, Lori, will pick her up," Clyde said as he kissed me good bye and headed out dressed in his softball uniform. I waved good bye and settled in for my big day.

Later that afternoon Lori arrived to pick me up. She was expecting me to be waiting in the office lounge and planned to swing through Starbucks drive-thru on our way back home. But when she told the receptionist who she was there to pick up, the girl said, "Oh, Gerrie's right here."

Lori looked through the door behind the receptionist's desk where I was sitting in a wheel chair, wrapped in gauze bandages and slumped in the chair. I looked like a mummy. The nurse gave Lori a white paper bag with several medications for me to take, some post-operative instructions and cautioned her that vomiting after surgery was quite normal. Lori's eyes were wide as she took in all the details she could glean from my morning. Finally, Lori rolled me outside, settled me into her car, buckled me up, reclined my seat a bit and then began the drive home.

"I'm sure it looks much worse than it is," I told Lori through my bandages.

Her ashen face was punctuated with the alarm in her eyes. "Yeah," she gulped. "You could say that, Mom."

When we stopped at a stop light, other drivers stared at me, but I was so full of pain medication that it didn't bother me. Lori however was deeply concerned. On the way home she made the decision that she couldn't leave me in Clyde's care. There were too many pills in my white bag that had to be taken at specific times and my bandages and bruises scared her.

Clyde took one look at my battered face and fell apart. "What were you thinking?" he asked through tears. "You said this wasn't going to be like this. You said a nip and a tuck." He wiped his eyes and shook his head. "I loved you just the way you were. Why would you do this to yourself?"

I didn't have answers for Clyde, and I was sorry that he was angry and frightened. I went straight to bed and stayed there for a few days. Lori stayed right beside me, even sleeping on the floor beside my bed, worried that this had been a terrible mistake. She was concerned for my health and felt compelled to comfort her father as well. I wasn't in a lot of pain – it really did look worse than it was.

In a few weeks, all the stitches and bruising healed, and I loved my new look. Unlike most of my friends who wouldn't admit to having plastic surgery, I was eager to tell everyone about it and to recommend my wonderful Dr. Jasper. Many of my friends – yes many – have followed me to Dr. Jasper – and eventually my daughter, Lori, will be one of them. She has started pulling up her sagging neck and pushing back her laugh lines; like mother, like daughter.

Mirror, Mirror on the wall – I am my mother after all.

SNAPSHOT 22

I Can't Hear You

I can remember exactly where I was and what I was doing the day I began to lose my hearing. It was the day we bought the blue Volvo from Jim and Ginny. I was driving down a Michigan road, near Quincy, when right out of nowhere, I had a terrible pain in my ear. It was almost more than I could bear. Unlike other aches and pains of daily life, it didn't go away. After a series of tests a specialist diagnosed me with Ménière's disease, a disorder of the inner ear that can affect hearing and balance. The doctor treated me with medication and the pain went away. I didn't realize that this episode was the beginning of permanent hearing loss.

The first time I realized that I was losing my hearing was a few years later when Clyde's sister, Mae, mentioned that whenever she talked to me I was cocking my head to the left and leaning toward her with my right ear.

The next time Clyde and I and our daughter-in-law, Michelle, went to our local shopping mall, there was a wellness promotion that included a booth offering a free hearing test. Clyde took the test and he heard all the sounds; Michelle took it next and she heard all of them, too. But when I took the test, I didn't hear any of the sounds, not the high pitched ones or the low pitched ones or anything! So Clyde and Michelle took the test again, and as before, they heard all the sounds. I put the headphones on once more, and again, I heard nothing. Clyde and Michelle were convinced that I must be doing something wrong, so we did the test over and over again, until it was clear that I could not hear any sounds that Clyde and Michelle could hear.

I went to an ear specialist, who fitted me for a hearing aid. It was bulky, uncomfortable and not a fashion accessory I had ever hoped to blend into my wardrobe. But I made up my mind I would not be intimidated by having a brown hearing aid sticking out of my ear with my blonde hair. I knew a friend who was ashamed of his hearing aid, but I was determined that I could make the best of this and perhaps I could even encourage others with disabilities.

A few years later, I was sitting in the car with my friend Sherry and her little boy Josh. There was a newspaper on the front seat, and I picked it up when I noticed an article about Heather Whitestone, who was deaf. She was featured in the paper because she was competing for Miss America. I looked in the backseat at Josh and I said, "Josh! This girl named Heather is deaf like me. She's in the Miss America Pageant." Josh looked at me in wonder. "We're going to pray right now that Heather Whitestone is crowned Miss America." And right there in

Sherry's car, the three of us – little Josh, Sherry and I prayed for Heather Whitestone to be the first deaf Miss America.

Our family gathered around the television to watch the 1995 Miss America pageant, and we all thought Heather Whitestone was the prettiest and the most talented of the contestants when she danced in the talent competition. We prayed all the way through the competition, in anticipation of God answering our prayer for Heather. I was beside myself in excitement when she was named Miss America, and I even threw a big party to celebrate.

I was proud of Heather for not allowing her handicap to inhibit her from all the gifts that God had given her. She was willing to take a big risk to enter the pageant. I'd never heard of anyone doing this, and since I had the same affliction, I wanted it for her. Even though I've never met Heather personally, I feel that she's been a mentor to me.

Losing my hearing was a difficult challenge for me, but I knew it was hard for everyone. My heart went out to children who couldn't hear their friends, or young parents who couldn't hear their children's laughter. Somehow it seemed to me that if someone like Miss America could be deaf, suffering a hearing loss could seem less tragic, less limiting and less of a disability to others with a similar affliction and more like just another life challenge.

My hearing aids have become a significant source of answered prayers for me. It seems I'm always asking God for something regarding my hearing aids.

Several years ago, I was going on a speaking tour to Russia and the day before we were leaving, I couldn't find my hearing aids. I began to pray in desperation for God to help me find them. I searched every drawer, closet, shelf, pocket, the car, everywhere! But I could not find them. My friends Sherry and Lynn came over to help me look.

I was so distraught. The trip to Russia had been planned for a long time, and it would be nearly impossible for me to be an effective speaker if I couldn't hear. I was running out of time to find them; we were leaving in the morning.

Lynn said empathetically, "Gerrie. We will find them."

"I've looked everywhere," I told her. "They are gone." I threw my hands up in despair. "I've been praying and praying, but I can't find them." I was so discouraged.

Lynn was determined. "We're going to pray again and then we're going to find them."

So together, the three of us prayed for God to help us find my hearing aids. Lynn and Sherry began searching through all the same places I had. They looked everywhere, even the refrigerator. Sherry went out to the car, and Lynn followed her out there while I sorted through a large drawer in my dresser one more time. All of a sudden I heard a scream. Lynn had found them in the car. They were lying on the metal strip of the threshold of the driver's side door.

That's when I remembered that I had taken my hearing aids out so that my hairstylist could spray my hair with hairspray. I remembered them in the salon, but when I got in the car to come home, I laid the hearing aids in my lap. As I was gathering my purse, sunglasses and keys, I forgot about them when I stepped out of the car. How amazing that instead of falling out on the ground when I left the car, they landed on this metal strip in the doorway and stayed there as I climbed in and out of the car. Taking them out and then forgetting about them when I got home was a foolish thing to do, but for me, it was just one more episode of my love/hate relationship with my hearing aids.

Recently my doctor prescribed a new high-tech hearing aid, with settings for conversation, telephone and television. I was so pleased with the clarity of sound, and I started noticing noises I hadn't heard in a very long time. So when I started driving to the grocery store with the sunroof open in my car, I was thrilled to be able to hear the birds sing.

"Thank you, Lord," I said out loud in the car, "I can hear the birds singing again." The birds were chirping and singing, and it was wonderful to feel so connected to nature once again. How long had it been since I'd heard birds so clearly? Their song was chirpy and persistent; and I felt blessed to be hearing their spring concert, until I looked back to change lanes and discovered that the chirping birds were perched on the back seat of my car! I had two live sparrows inside the car with me!

I'm not sure what I was thinking, but I slammed on the brakes and then made a sharp u-turn in the middle of the road. I needed Clyde to rescue me. I raced for home with the little brown birds in my backseat chirping away. I guess they were enjoying the ride because they just kept chirping louder and louder.

When I pulled in my driveway I hopped out of the car, yelling for Clyde. "Help me! Help me!" I called. I opened the back door of the car and begged the birds to leave.

"Shoo! Shoo!" I kept fanning my arms and swinging the door back and forth, trying to get the birds to leave. "Please little birds just fly away."

Clyde came running, wondering what the trouble was just as the birds took flight and flew out of the sunroof and into the tree beside the house. I let out a shriek of delight that my crisis was finally over, while Clyde laughed at the perky little sparrows who continued to chirp at me. I will always think of that grocery buying trip as one that was really for the birds!

My hearing loss eventually spread to both ears. It's a severe loss, but with the newest hearing aids and specialized telephones, I can hear relatively well. I am also blessed to be surrounded by Clyde, my daughter and daughter-in-law, who speak up to tell others who talk behind me that I am unable to hear them. Our family and close friends usually remember to choose social gatherings at locations without too much background noise.

Recently my grandson, Nathan, was planning a family event in Southern California for us and sent an email to all who were planning to attend that warmed my heart. It read: "I know a beautiful and quiet spot on Capistrano Beach that has killer fire pits right on the water. Not too noisy for Grandma. We should all get together for some serious s'mores action right at sunset."

Having hearing loss is not fun. I often get words mixed up like meet and heat, run and gun, more and four and cause my sentences to mean something totally different to me than the speaker intended. But, don't feel sorry for me. By keeping my sense of humor and my faith, I have seen God use my deafness to bolster faith and develop sensitivity in others.

My hearing loss has brought me frustrations and blessings. But more importantly, it has also provided me with some great friends. Ed and Gail are my local audiologists who have become good friends. I'm sure I have far more appointments than their average patient, but no matter what my hearing problem is or what adjustments have to be made to my hearing aids, Gail finds an appointment time for me right away. I've learned that audiology appointments must be planned into my routine, in order to hear. Ed and Gail make those necessary interruptions in my busy schedule easy and

As my hearing has deteriorated, Ed has been pro-active and provided me with great care. It seems like I pray to be able to hear, and Ed makes it happen. He selected specialized hearing aids that have significantly improved what I can hear. Ed helped me obtain a special telephone for deaf people, which allows me to hear much clearer conversations. Whenever I need new hearing equipment, Ed and Gail make sure that whatever I'm buying will last a long time. The newest, high tech hearing aid that Ed recently fitted for me should last forever – if I don't lose it.

SNAPSHOT 23

Lost At Sea

Nothing makes me more proud than my grandchildren, especially when I can see them using their faith to guide them through their lives. Whether it's a major crisis or an everyday task, God is at their side. One of our family's most frightening tests of faith happened to my oldest grandson, David, when he was a college student.

David, a student at Indiana Wesleyan University, wanted to change his major to International Relations. This required that David study abroad for a semester. David wasn't interested in studying in just one country, so he enrolled in a semester at sea through the University of Pittsburg. The semester at sea appealed to David because he and about 600 other college students would be studying on a huge cruise ship, traveling around the world to visit several countries and cultures. The ship would leave Vancouver B.C. and circumnavigate the globe, stopping at ports around the world.

The ship was about five days out, headed for South Korea, about 650 miles south of the Aleutian Islands when the 591 foot Explorer was caught in a fierce storm with 160 mph winds. The waves were 60 feet high, and the ship was tossed about in the violent storm. A huge wave crashed through the window of the bridge and the ship lost all power. The students, teachers and crew were helpless to navigate the ocean in the storm.

In the dead of night, David was awakened by the blast of repeating marine sirens – Baooga! Baooga! An alert message followed that announced, "All passengers put on your safety vests, and go to muster stations. This is not a drill. Prepare to evacuate."

David had about two seconds to react. He grabbed his life vest, his shoes and his Bible as he hurried to the muster station where he waited for more direction from the captain. There he learned that the storm had caused severe damage to the ship. They had lost engine power, but the ship could communicate via satellite. The storm raged on, and David could see the sea water wash over the port hole window with a surreal green glow. The vessel was bobbing back and forth in the wild 60 foot waves, crashing into the 60 foot valleys on the sea.

David recalls the next nine hours of being crushed into the muster station with the other passengers as a telling test of faith.

David:

When I heard the sirens and the warning to prepare to evacuate, I thought, "I might be dying right now." I was completely cognizant that this could be it. And I knew that I could either panic or have a spirit of prayer. As I grabbed my Bible and headed toward the muster station, I knew that I wasn't alone; God was with me.

I hurried along the dark, narrow halls toward the muster station thinking, "I have to be strong." I could hear people screaming and crying, and the potential for panic was hanging in the air. When I arrived at the muster station, I found a spot along the wall to sit down, opened my Bible and began to pray. It was there that I made a decision to hold on to God because everything else around me was moving, sliding, falling or churning. I didn't know where else to look other than to God, and that gave me peace as I waited to see what would happen next.

I truly believed God would save us. We were all bunched together, and people were falling on each other as the ship crashed on the giant waves. It wasn't chaotic. People were nervous, laughing uneasily in the jolting, uneven cadence of the ship. The Explorer – a 591 foot cruise ship - was within 15 degrees of capsizing on either side. The captain could do very little except try to manually keep the ship headed into heavy sea. We were still afloat, even though I could see the water washing over both sides of the ship, but we weren't sinking, and that was enough to keep me optimistic. Together, we all waited to see what was to come next. Evacuating the ship seemed like a very risky option with over 681 students, 113 instructors and 196 or more crew members. As the Explorer continued to crash up and down the towering waves, I knew our lives were in peril.

After about nine hours of sitting in the muster station, the storm calmed down, and the engineer was able to get one engine back up manually. U.S. Coast Guard aircraft and vessels were dispatched to guide us to Hawaii. The damage to the ship was significant, and we didn't know if we would be able to continue on our voyage. The library was ruined, the electrical equipment severely damaged and a grand piano lay in pieces on the floor. Many of the students wondered if our semester would be cancelled when we arrived in Honolulu. Some had no interest in continuing, regardless of what the university offered.

When we were released from the muster station, I found my friend Rebecca who had a satellite phone. "Rebecca," I said. "I'll pay you whatever I have to, but I have to call my parents. They can't hear about this on the news; I have to tell them I'm all right."

I placed the call, and Mom and Dad both got on the phone at the same time and were so excited to hear me. Before any more seconds ticked off, I interrupted them with, "Mom, Dad," I said crisply. "This isn't a happy phone call, and I can only talk a minute. I just want you to know that I'm okay. I'm alive, but my ship has been damaged, and we are on our way to Hawaii. I need you to pray..." and then the phone broke up and I lost the connection.

My parents started a prayer chain around the United States. People prayed for the disabled Explorer to make it safely to Hawaii. When we arrived in Honolulu, I was interviewed and featured on Good Morning America and NBC news. Eventually I was able to continue my semester at sea and earn my degree in International Relations.

I don't think anybody knows how they will handle a near-death experience until they do. A lot of "heart testing" happens when you realize that your life is about to disappear, and you immediately jump to what is of value to you. The night that I grabbed my life vest and shoes and then reached for my Bible, I realized that my faith in God was bigger than the crisis at hand. And regardless if I perished or not, I could not I abandon my trust in God. That's who I am; that's part of my heritage—

trusting in God is the natural response to any crisis in my family.

SNAPSHOT 24

Holy Nudges

My friend, Fizzy, is a remarkable woman in many ways. I met her when she came to our church and my first impression was, "What a classy lady." In her 80's, Fizzy looks and acts much younger. She is active in several organizations, loves to travel and dresses like she stepped out of a fashion magazine.

Fizzy is extremely fit and even went hiking in Peru, to visit the Inca ruins at Machu Picchu a few years ago. It was there that she fell and broke her hip, but in that remote part of the world, she walked on it for five days before she was able to obtain medical attention.

Shortly after that Fizzy had both knees replaced, yet three months later she accompanied Clyde and I on a trip to Israel, where she walked every step of the 16 day tour. God has blessed Fizzy with a positive spirit no matter what, and it's contagious.

But what I admire most about Fizzy is how she listens for God. Fizzy prays with faith, but she also listens in faith. I have coordinated nine travel tours to the Holy Land. Visiting the sites where Jesus walked is a spiritual experience that I cherish with each tour. A few years ago, my grandson David wanted to go to Israel with our tour, but as a college student, he couldn't possibly afford the cost. Fizzy knew that David wanted to go, and she and I prayed that somehow God would provide a way for David to come with us on our trip. I'm going to let Fizzy tell you what happened next.

Fizzy:

I believe that God answers prayers and that He answers them in many ways. When He wants me to be an answer to prayer, I receive what I've come to call, a "Holy Nudge." It's when I feel God calling me or providing me with a way to help.

I love the Mills Family. They are a spiritually-rich bunch, and all of Gerrie and Clyde's children are involved in ministry of one sort or another. I have come to know each of their children and admire the tenacity of their faith. It's a solid commitment, and God is the center of their world. The Mills grandchildren are wonderful young people, and like most pastors' kids, are not showered with a lot of material things. When I found out how much David wanted to go to Israel, I prayed with Gerrie that God would provide this big sum of money for David's tour fees. I felt confident that God would answer our prayer, but I didn't know how.

As Gerrie left my house that day, I hugged her good bye and waved as she drove home. I stood in my driveway a bit, and I kept thinking of David, such a handsome young college man who loved the Lord with all his heart. Touring Israel would be a wonderful experience for David, and I knew he would take advantage of every moment along the way.

As I walked back toward my front door, I stopped at the mail box, turned the key to open the flap and gathered a handful of envelopes from the slot. I went in the house and tossed the mail on the table in the entryway. I checked my answering machine, let the dog outside, poured a glass of iced tea, and then grabbed the mail to look it over outside on the patio. I relaxed in my favorite patio lounge chair, took a sip of tea and began to sort through the letters – a bill from the electric company, a flyer for a new plumbing service, coupons for a big sale at Macy's and a beige envelope with a return address from an investment firm.

I tore open that beige envelope and a quarterly dividend check floated into my lap. It was from an investment I'd made years ago. I was stunned to find a check for exactly the amount of money Gerrie and I had just prayed for to pay for David's trip. I thought about Gerrie and I just minutes before, asking God to provide a way for David to go on this trip, and now, unexpectedly, I received exactly that amount of money. Instantly I felt a Holy Nudge; God had answered our prayer.

I was blessed to provide David with the funds for the trip, but he in turn provided the highlight of my trip to Israel that year. When our group was touring the Shepherds' Church, David slipped in ahead of us as we were wandering the grounds. He loved the acoustics in the church and began singing softly to himself. David has a rich tenor voice and sings professionally. The acoustics in the church are well known, and his voice was loud, almost like it was being amplified. My daughter, Robin, heard him, and she grabbed me by the arm to pull me into the church to hear him. I knew immediately that it was David, and I ran outside to gather the rest of our tour group. It was such a special musical sound; I wanted everyone to hear it. Our group hurried inside the church, but we could hear him before we even entered the church. David was singing such a beautiful psalm, and all 60 of our tour group stood there in awe. God's spirit moved in every person listening that day in a way that you go to Israel praying will happen. It wasn't just a tune David sang, but a prayerful song of praise to our Lord.

I was honored to pay for David's tickets and humbled by how God was using me to further the faith and calling of this dynamic man. God moved in David's heart that day and it lead him to become a dual citizen of the U.S. and Israel. He obtained a Master's degree from Tel Aviv University, and at the time of this writing. is serving in the Israeli Army. I had experienced answered prayer before, but being nudged by God this way was exciting.

And then it happened again!

When Gerrie was discussing writing her first book, Oy Vey, Such a Deal, I was very enthusiastic. I thought that it was important for Gerrie to tell her stories so her grandchildren and other generations to come would know their history. Gerrie spreads God's word everywhere she goes, and she does it through retelling of her experiences. I knew that if Gerrie wrote a book, it would be unique and different from other stories of faith. Her biography is filled with adventure, romance, faith, life challenges and how to overcome them. I thought it was very important for her to write them down so others could grow the way that she could see herself growing.

But, as Gerrie explored the costs of preparing a manuscript, hiring an editor and going on book tours, etc. she was concerned about the costs. So we prayed that God would provide. When God didn't answer immediately, Gerrie thought maybe it just wasn't God's time for her book to be written, but I disagreed. I was adamant that Gerrie's stories needed to be told. In fact, I got rather cross with her about procrastinating! And then I received another Holy Nudge, and I invested in Gerrie's project. As a result, Gerrie traveled all over the United States with her book and hundreds of people have accepted the Lord through her stories of faith.

The Mills family has blended me into their lives. There is so much joy in that family, and they are continuously laughing and having fun. They are all fiercely committed to serving God and strengthening the faith of everyone in their paths. Together, we pray in anticipation of God answering prayers. My faith has grown in real joy through all the answers to prayer with the Mills family – even the ones we have prayed through adversity. I've never seen Gerrie and Clyde without prayer and faith, and they have been through plenty of challenges that would shake anyone.

SNAPSHOT 25

Reggie

Back in Quincy, a little girl named Reggie showed up at church one day. She was the youngest of four children and decided on her own that she wanted to start coming to church. She found a neighbor, who attended our church, and asked for a ride to Sunday school. And just like that, this little girl became an active member. Reggie attended church services and activities whenever they were offered – Sunday morning, Sunday evening and Wednesday night, along with Vacation Bible School, church camp and youth conferences. I didn't know too much about her, but I enjoyed watching this little girl live for the Lord. What I didn't know was what a big difference being part of our church family made for Reggie. To explain more, I've asked Reggie to tell you in her own words.

Reggie:

I don't know why I decided that I wanted to go to church, but one day I made that decision, and I found a neighbor who would take me to a little church in rural Quincy, Michigan, where I met Miss Gerrie and Pastor Clyde. I accepted the Lord under Pastor Clyde's wing, and he baptized me in the new church sanctuary. I met Gerrie's son, Tim, at school in Science class during the sixth grade. I remember seeing Tim at church on Sundays, and he was always coming up with goofy ideas and activities, like trying to fit as many kids as possible in the same pew. Church was a place where I always fit in and where I felt loved. I learned to pray there, to believe that God loved me and could direct my path throughout my life.

Miss Gerrie had the most amazing influence on me. I came from a very poor family. My father and my mother both worked in a factory, and we had very little money. My mom canned garden vegetables and fruits, and did all she could to save money, but financially we had a very rough road. Miss Gerrie never made me feel like I was poor. In fact, it was just the opposite; she made me feel special. Each Sunday Miss Gerrie would welcome me with a huge smile. Even as a little girl, I knew Miss Gerrie was different. She had a way of making me feel like I was the most special person in the whole church.

I never once told Miss Gerrie that we were poor. Yet, whenever there was something that I needed for a church event, she would tell me, "We will make sure you have..." whatever it was I needed. She arranged for me to have church camp fees and other church activity costs, but nothing stands out in my mind more than the purple jersey that Miss Gerrie provided for me so that I could play on our church softball team.

I didn't realize until I was older that Miss Gerrie took the pressure off of me to ask my parents to pay for anything. She made me feel just like all the other children in our church. She encouraged me in my faith and taught me to live for the Lord. She taught me to dream big dreams and to count on God to help me through everything. I vividly remember the day when she casually mentioned, "Reggie, I think you should go to a Christian college." I was in high school and hadn't really thought much about college. But Miss Gerrie planted that seed of possibility in my mind.

And then during the summer between my junior and senior year of high school, my father was suddenly transferred from Quincy to a new job in Indiana. All of a sudden I was starting a new school in another state. This was 1978 – long before email, Facebook or free long distance telephone calls. I didn't get to say good bye to my friends at school or church – I just didn't show up one day. And I lost track of everyone in Quincy at school and at church and even with the entire Mills family that I had grown to love so much.

But I didn't lose track of what I had learned from Miss Gerrie. I spent a lot of my senior year with the school guidance counselor, applying to colleges and for scholarships. No one in my family had ever gone to college, and my family certainly didn't have any money for me to go to college, but with Miss Gerrie's encouragement in my mind, I enrolled at Indiana University.

After college, I launched a successful career as a real estate broker, and I ended up living in the Virgin Islands. I returned to Michigan to look up some old friends, and through Facebook I found the Mills Family.   I was recovering from a health scare, and I had sold my business, feeling restless and off course. My faith was there, but unlike when I was a child going to church with Miss Gerrie, I didn't feel God's direction in my life.

I felt compelled to reconnect with Miss Gerrie and her family. So much so that I loaded up my belongings and moved to California, to the same little community where Pastor Clyde and Miss Gerrie lived. And again, under Pastor Clyde's wing and Miss Gerrie's affirmation that God had a plan for my life, I learned to live for the Lord all over again. I was right – just being closer to

Miss Gerrie and Pastor Clyde made me able to sense the direction God wanted me to go.

I rented a little house, and I loved my new life in California. I became involved at a church where Gerrie's daughter, Lori, and her husband pastored. I was active in children's ministry and threw myself into a flurry of activity. I toured Israel with Gerrie and her family. Walking where Jesus walked, hand-in-hand with a Jewish woman, was a remarkable experience that touched me deep inside my soul. My love for the Lord increased with each step along the tour.

We returned to California, and my faith and excitement in the Lord blossomed. Until one day when I woke up blind in one eye. It was devastating; I couldn't drive anymore. Gerrie and Pastor Clyde chauffeured me to treatment and everywhere else I had to go since California is a state filled with freeways and very little public transportation. Miss Gerrie encouraged me with, "We walk by faith, not by sight," and I held fast to her encouragement, believing that I didn't need my eyes to see, but just my faith to feel. She assured me that somehow God would use me despite this condition.

I was in California for about a year, undergoing treatment and still restoring my faith. Pastor Clyde and Miss Gerrie were such great support for me, but I knew that I needed to find a way to live independently despite my condition. It was a little conversation with Gerrie one day that opened my eyes to what I needed to do. "You really need to think about living in a place where you can walk," Gerrie told me. Immediately I thought of Charleston, South Carolina, a city that I loved, and a place where I could walk everywhere I needed to go. I knew that Miss Gerrie was right. I couldn't live counting on others to take me everywhere. In order for me to continue to thrive, I had to live where I could be independent, and that wasn't a small town in Northern California.

Within a few days, plans simply fell into place. God was giving me a clear direction as friends helped me pack up my life in California and move it to Charleston with every challenge of the move arising, only to be solved in faith. Even moving my

Cocker Spaniel puppy (who Gerrie had appropriately named "Quincy") turned into an easily solved problem when a friend volunteered to fly to California and drive me and Quincy back to South Carolina.

Today, I love my life in Charleston. Thanks to things like Facebook and email, I remain in touch with the Mills family. I am actively involved in a Christian church in Charleston, and I am heavily involved in fund-raising for children's projects for the Boys and Girls club. My life has been changed twice by Miss Gerrie and her family, first in Quincy, Michigan as a wide-eyed child of faith and again in Northern California as a blind adult looking for God's direction.

SNAPSHOT 26

The Survivors

My friend Anna is a survivor. No matter how tough the times, Anna focuses on problem solving and getting through whatever the challenge. But in the recession of 2008 Anna was faced with devastating financial ruin, the same as thousands of other Americans. I've asked her to tell her story of facing a most difficult challenge and how she prevailed.

Anna:

My husband and I ran a successful trucking company in Northern California and we enjoyed a very comfortable lifestyle. We owned a large, beautiful home, drove new luxury cars and vacationed at five star resorts. In 2008, when we returned from a vacation, we learned that we had lost a huge trucking contract that we had planned to take us through the next three years. Overnight we went from a five figure monthly income to virtually no income at all.

I didn't panic. I believed that God would see us through the hard times, just the same as He had other challenges I'd faced. My husband, Bill, began to look for other work for the company, and I continued to teach belly dancing and host church events at our house. We hosted Bible studies, missionary presentations, and ice cream socials – all sorts of church-related social engagements.

We had some savings, but with no income, it didn't take long for that to be eaten up with mortgage payments, insurance, car payments, and regular household expenses. Bill kept looking for work, but it seemed like construction had just suddenly halted, and there was no work to be found. Bill and I prayed for work, but none came our way.

My father passed away, and while most of his estate was tied up in a trust fund that I couldn't access, I did receive some money that was quickly spent to pay our truck drivers' back pay and other business related expenses. Within a few months we were falling behind and desperate to figure a way out of this mess. We had been working with a company to help us get a modification on our mortgage, but after months of negotiation we were disappointed to learn that we would not qualify. Then one day after Bible study was over, when I walked the ladies outside, I found a notice taped to the front door. It said our house was going up for auction. I was stunned. I didn't know what that meant, but I began to fear that Bill and I were going to end up living on the street. I pushed my fears aside and focused on God and looked forward to how He would answer my prayers.

It was embarrassing to realize that Bill and I had just a few days to move all of our things out of the house. Our friends rallied around us and came to help us pack. One friend had a trailer and we loaded all our belongings and moved into a small rental home in our community. We filled the garage full of boxes.

We hadn't even unpacked our household items at the new house when, in the middle of the night, our Mercedes was repossessed. Two weeks later Bill discovered that his treasured Corvette had been reclaimed in the early morning hours. That left Bill and I with a commercial gravel truck and a golf cart to drive. And no money.

It was shocking to suddenly be without any funds. When I opened the refrigerator and realized we had nothing to eat, I had faith, but I didn't know what we would do. God provided friends who showed up with bags of groceries. It was humbling to accept their charity, especially when I knew that these generous people didn't have extra money to be spending on our needs.

It was very hard to be without a car in California. Everyone drives everywhere. I continued to look to God for wisdom and kept doing whatever I could to make money. I didn't know it then, but slowly God began to put pieces together for us to make a financial comeback.

I kept teaching the belly dancing classes, and I had been selling belly dancing accessories at the classes. My supplier suggested that I try a few other items, and soon I was also selling scarves, sundresses and belts. When summer arrived, a Farmers' Market opened, with open air booths in a parking lot in our community. I decided that I would try to sell more of my wares there.

I loaded the golf cart as full as I could with sundresses, scarves, belts, jewelry and skirts; I looked like something from the TV show Sanford and Son. I didn't know what God's plan was at that point, but I clung to His promises and headed to the Farmers' Market. With my skirt billowing in the breeze like Mary Poppins, I drove the golf cart through the upscale neighborhood with tears of embarrassment and fear pouring down my face.

As I schlepped off in the hot sun of the Sacramento summer, I kept thinking, "What am I doing at a Farmers' Market?" But I *did sell many items, and I met a girl who offered to share a space with me next time, so I could be in the shade of her tent.*

I kept selling my clothing line each week at the Farmer's Market, and I began to see this venture had possibilities. I borrowed money to buy a tent to keep me out of the scorching sun, and my supplier allowed me to take inventory without paying him in advance. Soon, I was a bona fide vendor, selling clothing and accessories, and I started making a little money. When the season changed I sold sweatshirts, continuing to sell enough items to get us through the month.

A few weeks after we started the Farmers' Market, it was clear that we had to get a vehicle. I didn't know how we would pay for a car. But someone gave us a loan for a used car, and now I could take more items to the market each week. Then one day I stumbled upon an opportunity to be part of a street fair at a local concert venue, where I was able to sell even more of my clothing and accessory line. When winter arrived I was invited to set up my booth in front of a salon and again, God was in our midst, and I was able to sell enough to get by.

Bill and I sold our wares in front of the salon through the holidays. Instead of melting in the heat wearing shorts, now I was freezing in the cold Sacramento fog wearing ski pants. The holidays provided enough sales to support us, but after December we were hardly making expenses. Just when I thought God was going to see us through with sales, they dropped off to almost nothing.

I thought about looking for a place to set up a boutique, but retail space was far beyond my meager budget. And then one day, Bill and I found a cute little spot in a remodeled grainery. It felt as if God led us right to the door of this quaint little storefront. We met with the landlord, and within minutes we had a spot to open Anna's Sweet Repeats & Boutique, an upscale clothing consignment and accessories shop.

Now I could see God working vividly to restore us. The landlord was also a Christian, and he agreed to rent to us with terms far more generous than we would have dared to ask. He required no credit check, no deposit, nothing in advance. This generous proprietor wanted only to give us a chance to recover our solvency. Gerrie's husband, Clyde, came and prayed with us before the shop opened, another pastor dropped by to pray with us, and so did many other Christian well-wishers. Since then Christians throughout our region are dropping by on a regular basis. Each day we share the Lord with anyone who walks through the door. Our boutique is used, almost daily, for people coming in who need a word of encouragement, for others who don't know God or for some who just want to pray with us. They also come in to buy our beautiful clothing.

Bill and I are paying our bills and building our inventory. We've even begun to think about expanding to include items for men and home accessories. Recently I was asked to be the feature in a community fashion show champagne dessert gala.

The final chapter of our trucking business closed when Bill sold his truck. I thought it would be painful but God had a plan. Bill's health had been compromised from the stress of being a business owner and the physical strain of driving a big rig. Closing his trucking business took most of the stress out of our lives.

Today we live a much different daily life that is better for us on a variety of levels. We live in a small rental home. Bill goes to the gym every day, and he volunteers as a senior personal trainer. He's living a happier, healthier lifestyle than ever before. He believes that losing the trucking company saved his life.

I enjoyed a very comfortable upbringing of country clubs and Cadillacs. For most of my life I didn't even think about spending money; I just spent it on whatever I wanted. Today I understand the value of a penny, and I am proud that I can live on a small income. God changed my perspective and gave me compassion for anyone in a struggle.

It was humiliating to lose everything, and very, very difficult to hang in there when things looked so bleak. But the whole experience forced me to look at life so differently.

God has shown me that life isn't about things – it's about putting God first and helping others. I think I had a heart for serving people before, but it wasn't enough. Today I am in awe of God and make a concerted effort to put God first in everything. I don't know what's next for us, but whatever it is I know that God will be there with me. Gerrie has been a great friend and support for me, praying as I walked through those dark days of losing my house, my car and my status. Her encouragement, prayers and optimism sustained me. Looking back, I can see that God used Gerrie to keep me focused and determined to survive.

SNAPSHOT 27

Strangers In The Holy Land

I've made several trips to Israel, but the last trip included the complications from the Iceland volcano eruption. Planes were cancelled, re-routed or delayed all over Europe. After a long day of waiting, hoping and praying in an airport in Germany, we were advised that we would be able to continue our trip into Israel in a few hours.

One of the girls on our trip was Roseanne. A few months before the departure of this trip, Roseanne developed breast cancer. The chemotherapy and radiation were brutal, and Roseanne was recovering from that treatment when we were scheduled to depart for Israel. At first Roseanne's doctor recommended that she remain home, and not travel. But she was so desperate to go to Israel with us that her doctor released her early so Roseanne could go along as planned. She was still suffering a bit from the cancer treatment, but she left for the trip with enthusiasm.

Roseanne had a friend who was also suffering from cancer, and Roseanne promised to put a prayer in the Western Wailing Wall, on that friend's behalf. It was a solemn promise for Roseanne, and she took it very seriously. As we sat in that waiting departure gate at the airport, Roseanne struck up a conversation with Heather, a girl from Israel who Roseanne discovered was a cancer survivor as well. Roseanne detected a bit of fear in Heather's voice as she talked about surviving cancer.

"I want you to meet our tour director, Gerrie," Roseanne told Heather. "She wrote a book about her life as a pastor's wife. She's Jewish too! You might find her faith encouraging, the way I did when I was in treatment."

As the tour director, whenever there is an irregularity on the itinerary, it's my job to make sure that everyone is comfortable and try to help solve any problems. I was busy checking up on all of our tour group members, but eventually Roseanne introduced me to Heather.

"I would love to get a copy of your book," Heather said. "Roseanne thinks it might be encouraging for me. I'm a cancer survivor, like Roseanne."

I had one stashed in my carry-on bag, always prepared to share my story. I gave the book to Heather, and we chatted for awhile before I moved on to check on other passengers. As the hours dragged on at the gate, Roseanne and Heather exchanged more information. Heather was meeting family for a celebration; Roseanne was going as a Holy Land tourist. Roseanne told Heather about the prayer she planned to put in the Wailing Wall for her friend, and she offered to also put one in the wall for Heather.

Finally, we were able to board our plane. As we were lining up, Roseanne and I said goodbye to Heather, knowing we wouldn't see her again. But God had a plan.

Ten days later, our tour was going to the Western Wailing Wall. It was a highly anticipated stop, with many of our tour group members eager to bring specific prayers to the wall. The Western Wall, as the Jewish people prefer it to be called, is located in Jerusalem at the base of the western side of the Temple Mount. It is part of the ancient wall that surrounded the Jewish Temple courtyard and it is considered one of the most sacred places in Israel. Honoring God with your prayers at the wall is a holy experience; God loves the Western Wall, and He appreciates being honored there.

Everyone takes their time at the Western Wall. It's a reverent occasion for prayer and connecting with God. Roseanne stood at the wall and prayed for her friend and for Heather to be healed of their illnesses. Then she put her two little folded papers with those prayer requests into the stones of the wall. As is customary, Roseanne began to back away, rather than turn her back to the wall.

As Roseanne backed up, she bumped into Heather, the same girl she had just met in the airport a few days before. The two women let out a shriek of delight. Then Heather saw me and cried, "Gerrie!" Together the three of us hugged and laughed at finding one another again.

"Heather!" Roseanne gave Heather another hug. "I just placed my note in the wall for you! I just prayed for you. And now you are here!" Roseanne was so blessed to meet Heather at such a special moment on the tour. Heather was laughing and marveling at the coincidence of meeting the same two new friends at this Holy place.

Was it coincidence? Or was it God's timing? Israel is a big country, and the women were not traveling on a similar itinerary. The likelihood that they would bump into each other is slim. Coincidence? God's timing? To me it's the very same thing. God wanted to bless those girls at the Western Wall and to speak to their hearts in a very special way. Heather's heart was full of joy and wonder as she walked the path away from the Western Wall. Blessings are never coincidence.

SNAPSHOT 28

Close Call On The Highway

My granddaughter, Aubrie, and her friend, Halley, bought concert tickets to see Tyrone Wells, a folk pop artist they both loved. To get to the concert, the girls had to drive about 200 miles through some of the scariest cities in California. It was all freeway, so both Aubrie's mother, Michelle, and Halley's mother advised the girls to plan to travel straight through to the concert and not stop along the way. Before they left, Aubrie came to Michelle and admitted that she was a little nervous about the trip. She really wanted to go to the concert, but traveling through cities in the Central Valley area, which are regularly featured on the news with crime reports, was making Aubrie a bit uneasy.

"Mom, will you pray with me before we go?" Aubrie asked Michelle.

"Of course," Michelle told Aubrie, and they prayed together that the girls would have a safe trip, that God would watch over them and bring them both back home safely.

Aubrie and Halley were excited to take their road trip. Halley plugged her iPod into her car sound system and the girls chatted as they headed south on California Highway 99. It was a Saturday, and the traffic was light compared to a workday afternoon. Halley relaxed behind the wheel, and the girls enjoyed their time together. They arrived at the concert right on time and by midway through the program, the girls were in the very front row, dancing to the music and enjoying the scene up close and personal.

When the concert was over, the girls headed back home, going north on California Highway 99. Halley knew that she would have to buy gas for the return trip, so when she came to Turlock, a community where she had visited before, she decided to pull in a major grocery store. Halley knew it was well lighted, and there was a gas station with easy access back on the freeway.

Halley got in the lane to exit at Turlock, remembering there were frontage roads that run beside the freeway in this area. It was very dark, but the roads were dry and there was no fog. Halley and Aubrie were laughing and talking when they came to a bit of road construction along the freeway, and then they noticed a single bright light coming in their direction.

"That's weird," Halley said to Aubrie. She thought it might be a motorcycle on the frontage road. But within seconds, the light became brighter, and it was getting closer very quickly. Halley knew that whatever it was, it was coming down the freeway straight at them.

Halley glanced over her left shoulder and swung into the center lane, just as a battered van with only one headlight roared past them at an extremely high rate of speed, missing them by inches. Aubrie and Halley both knew that they had narrowly escaped a serious head-on collision. They were uninjured, but both were shaken, especially when it was clear that the van was being chased by several police cars.

Was it Halley's quick thinking that saved them? Was it a near-accident? Was it a close call? Or was God reaching down to protect the girls? I believe God answered Michelle and Aubrie's prayers before the girls left that night. Yes, I know that bad things do happen to good people and that wonderful people like Halley and Aubrie are seriously injured or even killed in accidents. But when you see a near-miss, a close call or a vivid miracle, why not celebrate the hand of God, rather than the happenstance of luck?

SNAPSHOT 29

String Cheese At Costco

I am always ready and willing to share my faith. Last week, I woke up just like a regular day, and as I finished my morning prayers, I asked the Lord, "Please let me be an encouragement to somebody today."

I made breakfast, tidied up the house a bit and then Clyde took me to Costco, one of my favorite grocery stores. I needed fresh produce, and Costco always has a nice selection. I mentally made my shopping list, and since it was getting near lunch time, I thought I'd try all the samples at the demonstrator tables too.

I wandered down the aisles, amid the usual crowd of shoppers. The store was bustling with shoppers pushing carts up and down the aisles, while stock boys tried to keep the displays full. I wove my way in and out of the shopping traffic, trying a bit of hot spicy sausage, some disgusting, dry low fat brownies and a bubbly new flavor of cranberry juice, chatting with the girls preparing the samples and enjoying the carnival atmosphere of this wholesale shopping store.

I came around the back of the store, along the dairy aisle where a dark-haired girl wearing a white apron had a sampling of string cheese in little paper cups. She seemed to have an air of melancholy about her as she kept her eyes lowered and smiled weakly. There was sadness around her eyes, and I wondered why this beautiful woman might be so unhappy.

I took a piece of string cheese from her sample table, thanked her, and as I started to move along, she stopped me and said, "Excuse me."

I turned back toward her and smiled.

"May I ask you a question?" she said in a thick accent.

"Of course," I said, and I walked back to her. I noticed her nameplate said, "Mozhgan."

She hesitated and seemed a bit flustered, but finally she said, "I don't speak good English. I don't know what is this word."

I looked at the package she held, and she was pointing to the word, "string."

I said, "String." I tried to pull a string from the hem of my shirt sleeve. "String." But I couldn't get a thread to come loose, and Mozhgan looked at me in confusion.

"String," I said again. Looking around us for something like a dog food bag or other item that might be sealed with string. "Like thread, only thicker."

Mozhgan pointed to the word on the string cheese wrapper again. "What does it mean?"

I looked around again, trying to think of a way to explain it to her. Then I picked up another piece of the string cheese and pulled a tiny section from the top of the piece toward the bottom. It rolled down into a curvy loop, and I held it up. "See, cheese." I held up the big piece; "String!" I held up the dangling string of cheese.

Mozhgan's eyes lit up in understanding. "Oh!" she cried. "String! I know now."

"I detect a beautiful accent," I said to Mozhgan. "Where are you from?

Mozhgan blanched. I hadn't expected it to be a sensitive question. "My home Iran," Mozhgan said. But immediately she added, "But I am not bad person."

I continued to smile. "Mozhgan, I can tell that you're a nice person." I patted her hand and tried to assure her that I hadn't meant to upset her.

Mozhgan continued. "Many of my people are bad," she said in her broken English. "They are not good. Some are evil."

"I can see that you are not a bad person," I said to her again.

Mozhgan seemed to relax a bit. "You do not think I am bad? I am not the religion of my country." She smiled gratefully, warming up to me a bit.

Hmmm, I wondered. Maybe she knows the Lord. I nibbled on the string cheese, and another customer came by and tried a sample. The customer smiled and pushed her cart on down toward the yogurt display.

"Mozhgan, you've been very kind to me today." I said quietly. "I'm talking to you, a girl from Iran and you're talking to a Jewish girl from America."

"You're Jewish?" she said astonished that the traditional hostility between Jews and Iranians wasn't happening between us.

"Yes, I am," I told her. "And I love you, and God loves you. That's the way it should be."

I held my breath. Historically Jewish people and Iranians are fierce enemies. I wondered if she would continue to chat or send me on my way.

"You are Jewish?" she asked again, stepping back to get a better look at me.

"Yes," I said. And I reached out and hugged her. I don't know why God led me to take the initiative that way. It's not like I hug all the demonstrators at Costco!

She hugged me back, and we were both smiling. I sensed a profound loneliness in this beautiful young woman; she seemed so glad to have found a new friend. We seemed to bond immediately.

"I am glad you know that I not friends with terrorists," Mozhgan said.

"Tell me," I asked Mozhgan as another customer came by to try the string cheese. "How long have you lived in the United States?"

"Two years," Mozhgan answered, beaming. "I not like other ones." She seemed determined to change whatever preconceived ideas I might have about Iranians. "I know there's Jesus," she said confidently.

"Oh how wonderful!" I said with a smile. "I'm a believer too."

Mozhgan's dark eyebrows knitted together. "You said Jewish," she said in confusion.

"Yes," I agreed. "I'm a Jewish believer in Jesus. I'm a Jewish Christian."

"How can you be Jewish and Christian?" Mozhgan asked, eager to understand, but finding herself more confused.

"I was born into a Jewish family," I said. "In fact I wrote a book all about growing up Jewish and becoming a believer. Do you read?"

Mozhgan nodded. "Oh yes," she said, smiling as she handed a sample of her string cheese to another shopper. "I'm learning English letters and words that way."

"You can be Jewish and become a believer," I told her. "You can be from any religion and come to know God through Jesus. I'm going to ask Clyde to go out to our car and get a copy of my book for you."

"How much?" Mozhgan asked. "I want to read book, but how much does it cost?"

"Oh no," I told her still smiling. "It's my gift to you."

Mozhgan and I chatted a bit as we waited for Clyde to return from the car. Shoppers continued to interrupt us, trying the delicious string cheese and then moving on.

There was a bit of a lull in the crowd when I asked Mozhgan, "May I ask you a question?"

Mozhgan nodded again, "Yes," she said and smiled with her eyes and heart.

"Have you ever asked Jesus to come into your life?" I asked.

Mozhgan shook her head thoughtfully. "No," she replied and she hugged me again. "I have prayed and asked God for more faith, even today."

Then I said, "I want to tell you how you can have faith right now and have your heart filled with happiness."

Mozhgan was looking at me intently, focusing on each word I said. "I'd like to help you understand that Jesus can come into your life and you can know God," I said. "Would you like that?"

"Oh yes!" she exclaimed. "Yes!"

So right there in Costco, I began to explain how God loved her, and that she could pray and ask Jesus into her heart to be her savior.

"You can pray a simple prayer, Mozhgan and God will come into your life and fill you with joy," I told her. "He will give you contentment, peace and forgiveness."

"Can you write it?" Mozhgan asked. "I need you to write it for me."

I couldn't find a notepad in my purse, so I snatched a napkin from the table and wrote a simple prayer on it with my purple ink pen.

"Make letters." Mozhgan said. She pointed to the block letters on the string cheese package.

I looked at my cursive writing and thought, "I can't even read my own writing, how could Mozhgan?" I nodded, turned the napkin over and starting printing. Then I handed the napkin to her.

Mozhgan looked at the napkin and then at me. "Mozhgan, you can invite Jesus into your life right here in Costco," I told her. "He will fill you with joy."

There was another lull in the customer traffic and right there in the dairy aisle of Costco, a beautiful dark haired, dark eyed young Iranian asked Jesus to be her Lord and Savior.

"I asked God to give me a friend," Mozhgan said as she held tight to my hand. "He send me you!"

Mozhgan explained that she had been a teacher in Iran for 13 years. Her husband had suffered a brain injury in the war that changed his personality. He became violent and abusive and Mozhgan found her only option to be to take her son and escape to her father's home in the United States. Since arriving two years ago, Mozhgan had felt isolated and alone and confused about how to raise her son with two different cultures tugging at the boy's heart. She had become depressed and discouraged as she struggled to live in America.

"You know, Mozhgan," I said with conviction, "Jesus will make all the difference in your life."

Mozhgan was beaming, laughing and smiling such a bright smile. "God send you today. I pray for faith and God send you."

Clyde showed up about then with my book, and I was pleased to give it to Mozhgan. "I'll be back tomorrow," I told her, and with a final hug I went on to the produce department.

As we said good bye I found myself being impressed with the fact that Mozhgan had been relying on God in her struggles. She didn't have doubts about God at all. She knew that he had been taking care of her, guiding her and keeping her safe. She also seemed familiar with Jesus, but I knew that today she had began a personal relationship with Him.

I returned to Costco the next day, and when I rounded the corner to the aisle where Mozhgan was stationed, it was like seeing a different person. She greeted me with hugs and kisses, and she was so glad to see me. Unlike yesterday, when she was subdued and quiet, today Mozhgan was bubbling with the hope in her heart. We chatted awhile, and I promised to come back to Costco later in the week.

That day, our son-in-law, Mark, was attending a ministerial meeting where he received two DVDs from Campus Crusade. One was the Jesus film and the other about Mary Magdalene. Both were in Farsi! I took both DVDs to Costco, and Mozhgan was so grateful and seemed excited to continue our friendship. She told me that she had just recently transferred to this Costco location, and she and I both knew that God had put her in my path.

Mozhgan's spirits are high as she explores her new faith. "I have so many questions. So many questions," she said.

"Well Mozhgan, get your questions ready," I told her. "And I will introduce you to the others in the family. They serve in ministry at two different churches in our area. We'll see which church you like best."

Mozhgan smiled and nodded, ready for new adventures. She recently sent me a cell phone text message that I treasure. It read, "I know Jesus sent you to me. He want to tell me I not alone here. He sent me you. I now have hope."

When I read Mozhgan's text I thought about my prayer that morning before I went to Costco. I had asked God to help me to encourage someone that day. He had surely answered my prayer when I tried a piece of string cheese.

SNAPSHOT 30

My Seventy-Fifth Birthday

Birthdays have always been cause for celebration at our house. I think it goes back to my Jewish heritage and a culture that really didn't need a reason to celebrate. So when my 75th birthday was approaching, my daughter, Lori, planned a surprise extravaganza. Unknown to me, Lori coordinated our family to converge in Southern California for a combination Disneyland/Los Angeles birthday event. But I didn't know about the Los Angeles part, or the birthday part – I was just invited to go with the family to Disneyland, where I was looking forward to riding the California Adventure rides. There was no mention of my birthday when Lori invited me.

When Clyde heard Disneyland, he elected not to go along, but all the grandchildren were eager to take me air ballooning over California or sight seeing for celebrities at Hollywood and Vine. The only Northern California grandchild that wouldn't be able to attend was my grandson, David, who was a member of the Israeli Army and lived in Tel Aviv. It's so hard to all be together and not have David with us. He was my very first grandson and very dear to me.

The Northern California group of our clan flew with Lori and me into Long Beach, where my grandson, Nate, and his wife, Gemma, lived and that became our "home base." When we landed in Long Beach, we all went to a beautiful restaurant, where we were seated, looking at the ocean, watching the waves lap the sand and the palm trees wave in the wind. I felt so blessed to be sitting by the ocean that I love so much. It was the perfect beginning to our holiday, and I relaxed as I enjoyed the beautiful Southern California beach weather.

As I sat there, sipping my diet coke and laughing with the grandchildren, I heard a voice from the doorway behind me say, "Happy birthday, Grandma."

I turned around to see my grandson, David, standing there in the restaurant. I was so shocked! I thought David was in Israel! David was supposed to be on duty in Tel Aviv, not celebrating my birthday in Long Beach! I couldn't even move; my body felt like it was stuck in slow motion as I tried to make my way toward David to hug him. I was in shock.

David explained that he wasn't AWOL; his superior officer had given him permission to leave. He had some vacation time accrued, so he talked to his superior officer, a woman, who was expecting a baby.

"I have vacation time coming," David told her, "If you're going on maternity leave soon, when should I take it?"

"Take your vacation now," she told him.

David was stunned. "What? Now?" he asked in disbelief.

"Yes," she said. "Take it tomorrow if you want."

"Oh, good!" David told her. "It's my grandmother's 75th birthday, and I want to surprise her in Los Angeles."

"Flights are limited and very expensive," she warned David. "You can have the time off, but you won't be able to make it home. It's impossible to book those flights in 24 hours."

"Watch me," David told her, and David began to pray. He checked all of the on-line discount airfares he knew and continued to pray, hoping to be with me on my birthday. With only a few hours to go, David was able to locate a flight to Philadelphia directly out of Tel Aviv at a fare he could afford. But when that flight landed, there was a terrible snow storm and David's connecting flight to Los Angeles was cancelled.

David didn't panic or fall into despair. David walked around the airport and prayed for God to provide a way for him to get to see me on my birthday. Soon one flight to Los Angeles opened up and David was on it. Hours later he was tapping me on the shoulder to wish me a happy birthday.

No matter how old you are, you are never too old for a good surprise. And David was the best surprise birthday gift I've ever received. No one in the whole family knew that David was making the trip, except his brother, Nathan. David's mother, Lori, and I clung to David all day; we were both so glad to see this young man who we loved so much and missed even more. We all went to Newport Beach and rented bikes to ride on the beach.

Disneyland was on the agenda for the next day. The grandchildren took me on all the non-scary rides, and I enjoyed seeing all the different cultures enjoy "the happiest place on earth." I especially loved "Soaring Over California," a high tech simulated hot air balloon ride over the great state of California.

The children and I laughed all day, ate all day, and wandered the immaculately groomed grounds of Disneyland all day. That night as we watched the light parade, then the laser show and finally the fireworks, I couldn't help think that this was a magical place to celebrate my 75th birthday with the people that I loved so much.

The next morning I got up early, thinking maybe we would visit the beach or relax with a little shopping. I went downstairs to wait for the family to get up and get going, when a big 15 passenger van drove up. The driver was honking the horn and the van had large lettering all over the windows that said, "Honk! It's Grandma's 75th birthday" and "Happy Birthday Grandma." Patty, Gemma's mother, who is now part of our family, had ordered the van so the entire group could travel together all day. Lori had another surprise for me as she handed me a small hot pink mail box with lettering on the outside that said, "Gerrie's Way to LA."

I opened the tiny mail box to find little cards, each naming a tourist attraction in Los Angeles. I was supposed to pick one or two destinations for our group to tour that day. The cards named everything from shopping on Rodeo Drive, Famous Cupcakes, fresh fruit at Farmers' Market, riding the trolley at The Grove, Hollywood, and Matzah ball soup at Canters Deli. Being game for any adventure with family, I chose them all, and asked to add China Town on the way.

Our family tour group all climbed into the van and Nathan suggested that we stop at the Crystal Cathedral in Garden Grove, since it was on the way. The Crystal Cathedral is a beautiful protestant church, built during the 1960's. Millions of Americans have seen the church on the television broadcast, "Hour of Power," featuring Dr. Robert Schuller. The Crystal Cathedral is famous for the all-glass façade and an incredible $2 million pipe organ. The main sanctuary seats over 2,500 people, and it is considered a landmark in Orange County. None of the children wanted to stop at the church on our day of fun, but Nate spoke up, "Let Grandma decide." Cars were driving by and honking at the sign in the van window that read, "Honk! It's Grandma's birthday."

It was Saturday, and we wandered into the foyer of this beautiful church, taking in the magnificent beauty of the design. The sanctuary was roped off and there were several security guards on patrol standing in the sunlight that pooled onto the tile. We could hear the deep, rich tones of the pipe organ being played and thought perhaps the organist was rehearsing for Sunday services. Lori approached the security guards, and I could see her chatting and smiling and using chutzpah. I

Holy Chutzpah!

couldn't imagine what she wanted to talk to them about so earnestly when suddenly Lori skipped over the rope barrier and approached the organist. She spoke to him briefly and then I heard "Happy Birthday" being played over the pipes of one of the world's largest, most famous organs. What an inspiring way to start my birthday!

Our group walked outside to roam the park-like setting and view the various sculptures. There was a special one that caught my eye, a stunning marble creation of Jesus sowing the seeds. And it was from the feet of Jesus, that I called Clyde. Then with all the family standing at this statue, over the speaker of my phone, Clyde prayed for each of us, our children and grandchildren to use their gifts and talents and sow more seeds for Jesus. It was an inspiring prayer, standing there, surrounded by my family as I listened to Clyde pray for Andy who works in law enforcement, Mike and Ellen in ministry, Tim and Michelle in ministry, Mark and Lori in ministry and all of our grandchildren. I was humbled to realize that our family legacy is to use our lives to bring more people to Jesus.

Before I hung up the phone, Clyde expressed his regrets to David for not coming with me on the trip.

After that wonderful detour to the Crystal Cathedral, Nate bought my breakfast at McDonald's, and then we all loaded back into the van. I grabbed a diet coke, and we headed for Los Angeles, with a stop off in Chinatown. I was thrilled to try all those things in the "Gerrie's Way to LA" mailbox, but I was most excited to end the day on Hollywood Boulevard.

Lori's husband Mark, our driver, dropped us off around the corner from the world famous Hollywood and Vine intersection of Hollywood. To my surprise, Kellogg was filming a cereal commercial there, and I wiggled my way to the edge of the barrier for a closer look. Lori's youngest son, Jon lives in Los Angeles and is an aspiring actor. He was at my elbow, pointing out the various technical aspects of the commercial creation and explaining the process to me. It was fascinating!

Jon was whispering something in my ear, when he was interrupted by someone from the camera crew. And then I was

173

shocked when the director of the commercial asked me if I would like to be in his commercial!

I was so surprised, I didn't quite know what to do, but Jon and the other grandchildren encouraged me to give it a try. I agreed to enter the acting business but only if he would include the grandchildren too. It was a fabulous end to Lori's great adventure for my 75th birthday, especially when I received a check for my performance and saw the commercial on Facebook! Even Jon was impressed, since he has an agent, a stylist and a manager as he works his way into the entertainment industry, and all I had to do was show up.

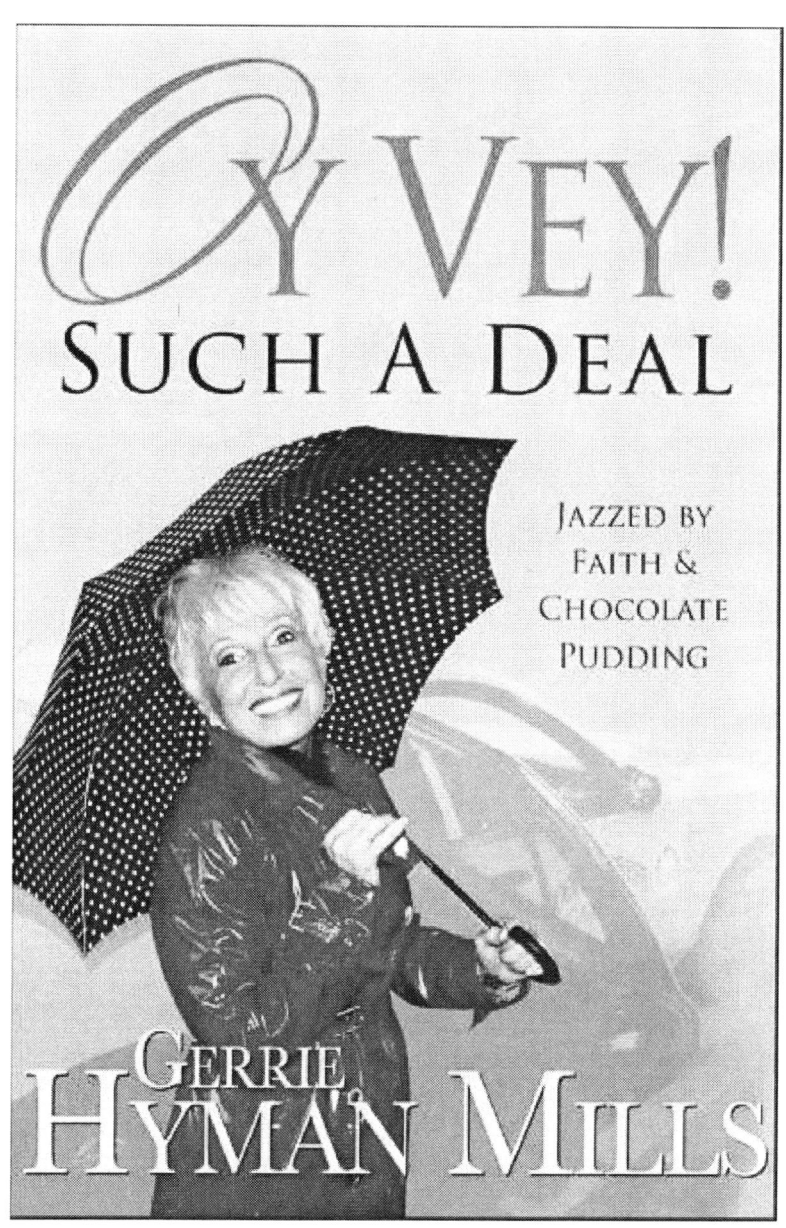

SNAPSHOT 31

An Unexpected Christmas Gift

A few months after I launched my first book, I was attending a Bible study luncheon and vendor event where I spotted some jewelry that I really liked. I struck up a conversation with the husband of the vendor as I looked over the many bracelets, broaches, necklaces and earrings on the table. I thought maybe he would trade me a book for part of the jewelry price, so I asked him if he liked to read.

"I'm not much of a reader," he admitted. "I spend most of my time working on my boat. But my wife is an avid reader. She always has her nose in a book."

"Oh," I smiled. "I wrote a book a few months ago. Would you be willing to trade this necklace, bracelet and earrings for a copy of my book?"

"Oh no," the man said. "I don't think so. Everything here is a cash sale."

"Well, I would be happy to pay for the necklace," I assured him. "But could you trade the bracelet and matching earrings for a book if I want the set?"

"Well, I don't know," he replied. He was already uncomfortable in this room filled with women and their chatter. Most of us were dressed up, and he was dressed in jeans and a T shirt with a sports logo over his heart. His muscles were bulging at the sleeves as he fidgeted in his chair. "I usually sell swimming pools, not jewelry."

"Well, what if I buy the necklace and the bracelet, and you trade a copy of my book for the earrings?" I persisted. My chutzpah was churning inside me, and I couldn't resist asking one more time.

"Okay," the man said with a grin. "I can do that. I'll give the book to my wife."

I ran to my car, grabbed a copy of the book, and came back inside to complete my deal. I was so excited to have this beautiful new jewelry, and I left that night feeling very satisfied with myself. I had no idea that God had a plan.

A few weeks later it was Christmas Eve. All of the family was coming to my house, and I had spent the whole day preparing until everything was perfect. I'd cleaned the entire house, prepared a wonderful meal, the table was set and pies were baking in the oven. I had a few minutes before the family would all begin arriving, so I sat down at the computer to relax and check my email.

I sipped my diet Coke as the computer loaded, and I clicked on my email icon hoping there would be messages from my sons who lived far across the country from me and wouldn't be coming to Christmas dinner tonight. I scanned my inbox and noticed an email from an unfamiliar address.

When I clicked it open, I received the very best Christmas gift possible.

It was a letter from the man who had traded the jewelry for my book. It read in part:

Dear Gerrie,

I don't know if you remember me or my wife, but we got to know your smiling bargaining powers when you recently traded us your book for three pieces of jewelry. I think I got the best bargain of my life and that was reading your book. I've never been an avid book reader. It is usually my wife that does all the reading, but I want you to know this book hit a cord for me that I can't explain in words.

I couldn't put it down and for me that is very unusual. I guess the cord you struck was me always longing to be part of the Christian faith. I haven't practiced any kind of religious caring in 25 years. I mean I've prayed quite a lot and always had knowledge that Jesus has been guiding many parts of my life, but I've never committed myself to the Lord. Your book has inspired me to learn more about Jesus... If you can recommend something for me to get started on this spiritual journey I think my life would be the better. I'm tired of this feeling that all I do is work and acquire things and yet I always feel this great emptiness.

What an incredible Christmas blessing to me! Of course I had all sorts of resources to share with him, and I replied right away. This man's thoughtful, heartfelt email was the best Christmas gift I had ever received. It was especially sweet because I was sure that it would also be the best Christmas ever for this new believer.

SNAPSHOT 32

Faith In Business

When I began planning this book, I wanted to include some of my stories from my first book, *Oy Vey! Such a Deal* This meant that I would have to buy back the rights from the *Oy Vey!* publisher; and I would also have to buy any books that the publishing house had in stock. Clyde and I are retired now, with very little disposable income. So we didn't know if this would be a good investment for us or not.

We discussed our options with our publishing friends, an editor, a financial advisor and all of our family. Everyone was enthusiastic about me writing a second book, but they also agreed that investing in books that were four years old was risky. All the family agreed to pray about it with us and finally, feeling confident that God was with us in this venture, Clyde and I decided to invest a sizeable sum. I called the publisher and asked them to email the contract, and I gave them my credit card number over the phone. A truck filled with the remainder of my copies of *Oy Vey!* was on its way.

My developmental editor, Cindy arrived just as I hung up the phone. As she opened her laptop on the desk in my office next to mine, I told her that I'd sealed the deal.

"We need to pray," I said. "I'm not sure how God is going to work out this project."

Cindy and I turned both turned toward one another in our swivel chairs, grabbed hands and prayed together as we did before every writing session.

"God," I began softly. "I just purchased my rights and all the copies of *Oy Vey!* It was a lot of money! But I did it with a purpose to share my stories with others. I want people to get to know You through my stories. I don't know what I'm going to do with all those books, Lord. You have to be the one to move the books. It's beyond me."

"Amen," Cindy and I said together, and we settled in for a morning of writing. But like many of our sessions, we had only worked for about a two minutes, when the phone rang. I answered to hear the friendly voice of, Patricia, a professor at both American River College and California State University, Sacramento.

"Gerrie," she said. "I've been looking for a new autobiography to use in my English classes, and when my eyes caught sight of your bright yellow book on my bookshelf, I thought 'That's it!' That's the autobiography I want my students to read."

"And Gerrie," Patricia asked. "Would you be interested in speaking to my classes about your life and your book? We can hold a book signing event."

I was stunned. I shouldn't have been. This is how God works. I had just purchased the books in faith. Within a few minutes, God had a plan in place to deliver them into the right hands.

When Cindy and I prayed, I honestly didn't think we'd have an answer within two minutes! But we did.

"Um, um, um," I gasped. "Yes, I'd love to!"

"Great, I'll get back to you with dates," Patricia said. She also gave me an address to send a sizeable number of books for delivery by next Friday.

Patricia's students purchased copies of my book to read for their class, and when I added up the money that came in as a result of those sales, it was nearly the same amount I had spent for the whole shipment of my books that I had to purchase (along with the rights to use my stories). Within minutes of making my investment, Patricia's phone call requesting to use my book in her class had enabled me to recover my investment, and I had secured the rights to my book!

Patricia offered an extra credit option for her students to meet on American River College's campus one evening to hear me speak. I was asked to share some stories from my life and answer questions from students who had read my book for the class. Since this was an extra credit assignment and outside of the students' normal class meetings, I wasn't sure how many students would show up. However, I was surprised to find the lecture hall filled to capacity with students standing in the aisle and outside in the hall.

The students' questions were insightful and reflective of a society that seems filled with wonder over spiritual matters. It was heartwarming to hear that they grasped the drama of being a pastor's wife and the complex issues involved in ministry. I was energized by their questions because I could tell they were sincerely from the heart. The students had numerous spiritual questions regarding peace, how to find eternal life, understanding God's will, and as I answered their questions, I was grateful for the investment that I had made. Many of them acknowledged that they had prayed the prayer that I offered at the conclusion of the book. It's a prayer to accept Jesus into your heart and life.

I think that's why so many people were there that day. They felt connected to something life-changing and wanted to share it with me. This speaking opportunity alone made the scary investment of purchasing my book rights and the remaining copies of *Oy Vey!* worth every cent.

SNAPSHOT 33

If Not Now – When?

My friends Anni and Tony visited our church a few years ago, and somehow I just knew that Anni and I would become good friends the minute I met her. There was this instant spark of connection between us as I introduced myself as the pastor's wife. They began attending regularly, and Clyde and I enjoyed getting to know Anni and her husband, Tony, a distinguished businessman in town, with a charming British accent.

Anni and Tony had married later in life, but they had met in Hong Kong as children. Anni was a Northern California native, while Tony, who was born in England, had spent most of his adult life in Australia. Remarkably, Anni and Tony rekindled their childhood friendship from two different hemispheres when they began to fall in love.

I've asked Anni and Tony to share their story of faith as they moved to our community and began to feel the Lord tugging at their hearts.

Anni:

Tony and I met when we were 11 and attended the same British school in Hong Kong. We were classmates for about four years until I left Hong Kong, and after that we didn't see each other anymore. We were not a couple as children, although later, as adults, we did confess to having a secret crush on each other.

Tony had spent most of his adult life working in business in Australia. We began corresponding by email and that relationship blossomed into marriage.

Tony:

I retired as a radio officer from the Merchant Marines and immigrated to Australia, where I entered the computer industry. Eventually I became a professor at a college in Brisbane. One day I received a surprise email from Anni, which led to chatting on the phone and eventually meeting her in San Francisco. As Tony Bennett sang that he "left his heart in San Francisco," I found that when I returned to Australia, I had left my heart there as well. I sold everything and moved to Northern California to be near Anni. To my delight, she agreed to marry me, and we decided to locate near her elderly parents' home in Sacramento where I could work in the real estate industry.

Anni:

Shortly after Tony and I were married, we went through a lot of distress with my family. My father died, and my mother had significant financial complications. There were so many decisions to be made, details to work out, and it was extremely stressful. Even with Tony at my side, I felt lost and filled with anxiety. I wasn't a practicing Christian; I worried about everything and felt completely unsettled.

Tony's real estate business was thriving in Lincoln Hills, California, the retirement community where my Mom and Dad had lived, and he wanted to move there. I felt far too young to be living in an entire city of people over 55, but reluctantly I agreed, still reeling from my father's death and all the turmoil that resulted. When we moved to Lincoln Hills, I told Tony, "We need to find a church."

Tony:

I felt myself nudged and pushed to come to the Lord. We moved to Lincoln Hills where my business was going very well. My sister, a devoted Christian, came for a visit. In the past whenever she had talked to me about God, I had resisted. But now, I felt awakened by her Christian wisdom, and something was kindling inside me. I looked at the prosperity in my life and felt that I had to give thanks for all the work and business I was getting.

So Anni and I visited Valley View Church, a congregation that met at one of the recreation centers in the Lincoln Hills retirement community. The people were warm and friendly, and worship was being lead by the music team, since the pastor was away on vacation. We visited a few other churches, with varying degrees of discomfort. It would have been easy to give up on Anni's determination to find a church, but my sister had left me with that seed of inspiration, and we kept looking. A few weeks later we visited Valley View Church again to meet Gerrie and Pastor Clyde, who had returned from vacation.

Clyde's style of preaching was extraordinary. He had such a commanding presence and was authentic and believable. His "John Wayne" persona confidently revealed the truth about God. It was wonderful, and Anni and I both felt that we were *learning so much about the Bible and how God was reaching out to us for a relationship.*

Anni and I kept returning to Valley View Church each Sunday, looking forward to Clyde's preaching. His message was always well planned and filled with Biblical integrity. Each Sunday Clyde would conclude with an invitation to call the Lord into our hearts.

Each week, Anni and I would hear Clyde's sermon, feeling sure the message had been written just for us. One particular Sunday, Clyde's sermon truly gripped our hearts. By the time Clyde finished, I was in tears. I didn't realize that Anni had been equally moved, but as the service closed, Clyde prepared his final words.

"Before we leave today, I invite you to ask the Lord into your hearts. If you haven't made that all-important prayer for salvation yet, let today be your day. God's word says, 'Today is the day of salvation. For whoever shall call upon the name of the Lord, shall be saved.'" Clyde looked out at the congregation kindly. "We pray this prayer every week, and I encourage you to ask the Lord into your heart today." Clyde paused for a second, and I felt as if his eyes rested gently on me as he added, "If not now, when?"

Those four words echoed in my mind. "IF NOT NOW, WHEN?" I thought, "What am I waiting for?"

Clyde continued. "Dear God, thank You for sending Your son, who went to Calvary's cross where He shed His blood and died, then rose again for me. By faith, I'm asking You to come into my life and forgive me of my sin. Make me the kind of Christian You want me to be. Thank you, God, for saving me."

I whispered the prayer to accept the Lord into my life as Clyde spoke it from the podium.

Anni:

Sitting next to Tony, I was not paying much attention to him. Instead I was hanging on to every word Clyde was saying. His question really got to me. If not now, when? He was so right!

What was I afraid of? I believed in the God that Clyde was preaching about, so why not now?

As Pastor Clyde prayed that prayer to accept the Lord, I silently prayed it with him. I felt my defenses melt, and tears ran down my face.

When Tony and I got home, as I put my coat away I said, "I accepted the Lord today."

Before I could get another word out, Tony said, "I did too." We were surprised to discover that we had been experiencing the same internal spiritual calling at exactly the same time.

Tony:

What a surprise to learn that our hearts opened at the very same time for the Lord to come in. The Holy Spirit had worked in stereo with us. We called Gerrie and Clyde, and they invited us to their house, where Clyde shared wonderful scriptures to solidify our commitment. I started reading the Bible, going to Bible studies, and getting into the Word of God.

From then on I immersed myself in the Bible, with books, commentaries and every translation of the Bible I could find. My lifestyle changed. Anni and I made new friends and became engaged in living our lives for the Lord. Our taste in music has changed. We began to listen to Christian music and to listen to the Lord speak to our hearts. As a result, our desires became different. Anni and I even went on two trips to Israel with Gerrie, which inspired more depth of study and knowledge of our Christian heritage.

Anni:

My new-found faith was connected to some things from my past. There was a time in college when all I wanted was a Bible. I had been in touch with God, but I truly didn't understand what Jesus was all about. I thought He was the son of God; I did not understand that Jesus was God or that I needed a personal relationship with Him. This concept was a huge understanding for me. Through Clyde's preaching and Gerrie's Bible studies I began to grasp that Jesus was God incarnate and that the only way to be saved is with a personal relationship with Him.

But the best part for me personally was the peace. I had always wanted peace in my life. But I had never felt peace. I used to worry a lot – about everything – but since the day I invited the Lord into my life, I have felt peace. Now I don't worry at all.

I thoroughly enjoy my friendship with Gerrie. That first day when I met Gerrie after church, she embraced me and said, "I think we are going to become very good friends." And she was right! Our walk with the Lord together is fun, lively and an adventure.

Gerrie and Clyde are such an opposite combination. Gerrie's the bubbly fashion plate, and Clyde is the quiet, reserved, theologian with a dry sense of humor. Yet they work in concert as only God can put a combination like that together. Their friendship and encouragement have changed my life.

Gerrie's faith has inspired me to turn everything over to God. Gerrie prays for everything – not just the big stuff, but for everyday things like lost sweaters or parking spaces. Gerrie's faith is strong, pure and innocent. When she invited Tony and me to lead a Bible study, it was her faith that dissolved my reservations.

I also have another special connection with Gerrie. When my father died, I learned that his parents were Jewish. The fact that my father never claimed his Jewish heritage confused me. This was a part of my history that was important to me. I felt that I had missed out on a whole part of my life that could have been very enriching. Then Gerrie took me to Israel and for the first time I felt as if I were at the beginning of the beginning, and everything was connected. We were two Jewish girls walking together along the streets where Jesus walked and I loved it. Oy Vey!

Tony:

Since we began leading our first Bible study, we have developed rich relationships within a devoted core of people who love the Lord. Anni and I team together to lead each class by researching and preparing lessons. I have always held Clyde on a pedestal for his strength of faith, integrity and devotion to the Lord. I admire how he puts his sermons together with days of study. He doesn't search the internet or copy and paste with a computer. Clyde writes his sermons on yellow legal pads, with Bible in hand, word by word prayerfully considered as the Holy Spirit works through Him. Even after his retirement, I can still hear the powerful words Clyde spoke in his sermons. He will always hold a special place in my heart for being the pastor who opened the door of salvation for me. .

As they retired, Clyde and Gerrie left us a huge legacy. Anni and I still serve on various church committees, we continue to lead our Bible study, Anni sings with the praise team, and I am playing the guitar for services. It is our lifestyle and calling today. It was the good times that brought me to seek the Lord, yet I will always feel that my salvation was another gift from God through Clyde and Gerrie.

SNAPSHOT 34

Behind Every Successful Pastor, There Is A Wife Praying

Clyde and I were happily retired when family members introduced us to Dr. Steve Babby, the District Superintendent of the Pacific Southwest District of the Wesleyan Church. Both

Clyde and I took an instant liking to Dr. Babby and his wife, Barbara, and we were surprised when Dr. Babby asked Clyde about pastoring a new church plant. The Del Webb retirement community of Sun City Lincoln Hills was being built, and Dr. Babby invited Clyde to consider becoming the pastor of Valley View Church of Lincoln Hills.

Both Clyde and I were quite happy in retirement, and it seemed so strange that the Wesleyan Church was interested in Clyde, since we had not served in that denomination before. But after prayerful consideration, extreme encouragement from our children who live on the West Coast and the earnest counsel from Dr. Babby, Clyde accepted the position.

For the next 10 years, Clyde and I served in building a brand new congregation, made up entirely of the over 55 generation, that lived in the Sun City Lincoln Hills community. Without the demands of Sunday School and children, this was a whole new world of ministry and as Clyde's administrative assistant, I enjoyed the challenges associated with an all-adult congregation. Dr. Babby and Barbara, were always available for help, if either Clyde or I needed it.

Dr. Babby's leadership was exemplary for Clyde and I. His wisdom was always guided by Biblical principals and laced with experience. He was a pastor's dream as a District Director. Dr. Babby recognized the need to interact with other pastors and actually arranged for all the District's pastors and their wives to attend a conference aboard a cruise ship.

Over those next 10 years, Clyde and I watched Sun City Lincoln Hills to go from the initial neighborhood of 100 homes, where we lived, expand to a large development of nearly 7,000 homes, across 3,000 acres. Valley View Church began in our living room, and eventually expanded into a lecture hall in the Lincoln Hills recreation center. Many people came back to the

Lord, or accepted the Lord during our tenure at Valley View and Clyde was thriving as a pastor and also a community member. But after our 10th year, Clyde and I felt called to retire, once again. Even a congregation without children has plenty of demands on its pastor. As we contemplated leaving the leadership of our church, it was sad to think of no longer belonging to that wonderful fellowship lead by Dr. Babby.

Clyde and I again counseled with Dr. Babby, about going back to retirement and he was encouraging in our quest to follow God's call. But the big question that loomed large on the horizon was who would follow us to pastor Valley View Church? Together, Dr. Babby, Clyde and I prayed that God would lead the way.

Barb and Joe Riley were planning to retire in the Del Webb community where Clyde and I lived. After 50 years in ministry and the last 15 years as director of the Kenya Evangelical Mission in East Africa, Joe was ready to resign his pastoral duties and the Del Webb Lincoln Hills community in Northern California appealed to both him and Barb.

Joe's idea of retirement was to continue to serve at a church, but his plan was to thoughtfully and methodically visit many churches in the area before settling into a church family.

Barb had been given a copy of my first book, *Oy Vey! Such a Deal* as a gift. She enjoyed it and insisted that Joe read it, too.

"If we move to Lincoln Hills," Barb told Joe, "We are going to attend their church."

Joe was agreeable to a visit, but he still planned to explore all the church options in our community.

But God had a plan and revealed it to Barb. "No, we don't need to visit other churches," Barb told Joe. "We are going to join this one."

Joe read my book upon Barb's recommendation, and he appreciated the values that Clyde and I use in ministry, but he still expected to take his time finding a new church home.

"I thought I would visit several churches," Joe said. "I wanted to sit under a good pastor and serve wherever I was needed. I intended to retire, slow down and enjoy our new home."

Barb continued to insist that their new church home had already been resolved. She had faith that God was putting a plan for their retirement in motion. Her prayers had always been to go where God called them, and in retirement her faith remained strong.

Joe and Barb came to Lincoln Hills to visit and attended our church. Joe liked Clyde's style of preaching, but he was still open to exploring other possibilities. Barb, however, felt a calling for both herself and Joe.

"This is where we need to go to church," Barb said to Joe, waving my book at him. "God has plans for us there." This insistent attitude was completely contrary to Barb's usual supportive role as Joe's wife. But she couldn't let go of the idea that Joe would be called to serve in a major way at our church. "We have to go to church there," she told Joe.

"No," Joe replied calmly. "We're going to look around a bit first."

"But we have to go to this church!" Barb defended. "I just know it."

"What are you doing?" Joe asked her. "Why are you so insistent?"

"We have to go there because someday you are going to be the pastor at that church," Barb told Joe.

Barb and Joe sold their home and moved to our little Del Webb community in Northern California. Joe still had plans to explore other churches, but he and Barb came to visit our church that first Sunday they came to town. From there, they jumped in and became heavily involved in various forms of ministry within our church. When Barb and I met, we struck up an instant friendship. We were both life-long pastors' wives, married to strong Christian men with shepherds' hearts, and we understood one another immediately. Our husbands were equally compatible, and since Joe wanted to serve at a church in retirement, Clyde asked him to take over a Bible study.

A few years later, When Clyde submitted his pastoral resignation, he asked Joe to consider applying to replace him. Barb's faith was honored when just four years after she met Clyde and I through my book, Joe became the pastor of our church.

"I really wasn't looking for a pastor's position," Joe laughed. "I figured 50 years in ministry was long enough. But this church is filled with sweet people, and I am enjoying it a lot. I told the church I'd give them 20 years, and then I would retire."

Barb just smiled and did her best not to say, "I told you so."

SNAPSHOT 35

We Plan, God Laughs

My granddaughter, Andrea, was getting married in San Diego, and all the family across the country wanted to be there. It was a great excuse to go shopping, and I found a dress that I liked, and if I stopped eating chocolate for a month and exercised a bit, it would fit me just right. In my exuberance to fit into the dress, I started doing Zumba and exercising twice a day with resistance bands. Somehow, I didn't resist right and tweaked my knee. The day we were going to fly to San Diego, I was limping my way to the concourse. Nothing was going to dampen my spirits about going to Andrea's wedding! Even though I was in pain, I felt jubilant because I fit into my new dress, and I was going to spend the next four days with my loved ones. The day before Clyde and I left for San Diego, we discovered that Wes and Carolyn, our life-long friends from New England, were going to be in San Diego at the same time. It was destined to be wonderful week.

All the family members coordinated our flights so the father-of-the-bride (my son Andy) could pick us all up at the airport in one trip. At the time Andy was a lieutenant in the San Diego Police Department, where he headed up the Criminal Intelligence Unit. The weekend of Andrea's wedding was also the tenth anniversary of the September 11th terrorist attacks at the World Trade Center and Pentagon. As head of the CI Unit, Andy's father-of-the bride duties were reduced to simple tasks like picking up family at the airport, while he kept his ear tuned to the police scanner. It was our daughter-in-law, Cathy, who was coordinating a fairy tale wedding for their daughter Andrea.

We all arrived in San Diego in the middle of the afternoon, so excited to be together again, laughing, hugging and looking forward to the big party that night which would kick off all the wedding festivities for the next three days. The party was scheduled to be at Andy's house where Cathy was busy preparing a feast for all the family and everyone involved in the wedding.

Andy squashed our luggage into the car and then we all piled in to go to Andy's house. But we didn't get far. As we started down the road, the traffic lights weren't working. Andy's police radio crackled, and Andy told us that it wasn't just stop lights. All the electricity was out in the entire San Diego area. As head of the Criminal Intelligence Unit, Andy went into high alert. This was an historic weekend of terrorist activity, and Andy had a responsibility to the people of San Diego to be vigilant about security. He had planned long in advance to be away from his office this weekend, but nevertheless, Andy remained ready to respond to any emergency.

Traffic was gridlocked. If cars were moving at all, it was at an extremely slow pace. We didn't know why the lights were out or for how long they would stay out, but it was clear that everything in San Diego was impacted by the power failure. Andy knew the back roads, short cuts and side streets, and eventually, we made it to his house.

A normal person would have cancelled a big party in these circumstances, but my daughter-in-law Cathy isn't normal. When we arrived at Andy's house we found Cathy cooking on the barbecue gas grill and re-designing her dinner to accommodate the lack of electricity. Andy walked in, and she handed him the role of barbeque chef, and he began turning the chicken and basting the pork. Cathy moved on to cut up the fruit and prepare the rest of the meal without electricity. I was struck by both of them being so cheerful and optimistic – Cathy, as she calmly faced the challenges of hosting a big party without electricity and Andy, with his ear tuned to his police radio, ready to run to the police headquarters, if needed. They were both peaceful and seemed determined to enjoy the weekend they had planned.

Andy was busy at the grill, but still playing host to a house filled with guests, when he groaned. The grill was out of propane gas. Cathy walked out to the patio, and quietly smiled at Andy.

"Got it handled," Cathy said to Andy as she walked over to a patio heater and pulled it apart. She fiddled with some attachments and then next thing I knew Cathy pulled out a propane tank from the patio heater and handed it to Andy.

"No problem," Cathy said with a confident grin and went back to fixing dinner.

As it began to get dark and the lights were still out, Cathy opened a big box of wedding candles and began unwrapping the hurricane globes.

"Oh Cathy!" I exclaimed. "We can sit in the dark. You can't light those beautiful pillar candles! They are so expensive!! And they're for the wedding!"

Cathy didn't skip a beat. She just smiled and said, "Mom, in cases like this, you've got to adapt." She put the candle into the globe and lit it to cast a whispery glow around the room.

Cathy unwrapped more hurricane globes and candles, lit them, and we placed them around the party. We enjoyed a wonderful meal with family and friends so happy to be together in this lovely setting. Many of the guests hadn't been able to attend the party simply because it was impossible to get across town. But eventually people began to filter in, and many of the guests did make it to Cathy's lovely dinner.

Andy and Cathy had arranged for all the family to stay at a beautiful French chalet in La Jolla. When it was time for Andy to drive us all over there, Cathy took one of those hurricane candles out to the garage to use as a flashlight, and she located her battery-operated Christmas candles. Cathy gave each of us a Christmas candle to take back to the chalet.

The next morning, the electricity had been restored to the city and reports indicated that the power failure was due to an operator error rather than a terrorist attack. Andy breathed a big sigh of relief. Since we could get around San Diego safely now, everyone wanted to go to the beach. My knee was still aching, but I didn't want to miss any of the fun. Andy picked us up, and I was thrilled to be sitting along the ocean again, watching the giant Pacific waves crash along the shore.

We had quite a crowd with us at the beach. Our relatives, the wedding party and many friends came to share the beautiful Pacific Ocean waves. The kids were splashing in the surf, riding boogie boards and playing in the water. Wes and his wife Carolyn were there, and before long Wes, who is just a few years younger than Clyde, was out there in the water, body surfing on the huge pounding waves. A big wave came up and Wes rode it in, and then another wave crashed to take Wes back out into the water. Wes and Clyde had grown up together in the water and were both strong swimmers. Wes was an avid sailor off the coast of Maine, so it didn't surprise me that he wanted to enjoy the summer surf in California. I could hardly believe Clyde hadn't jumped in the surf as well.

Clyde was standing on the rocks, taking pictures while the rest of the group was either playing in the water or sunbathing. Impressed with Wes being out there body surfing at his age,

Clyde began to think that maybe he would join Wes in the water. Wes was clearly having fun and so were all the kids. But as Clyde was watching Wes, he noticed that Wes wasn't swimming or riding waves anymore. he was simply being washed back and forth onto the beach and back out into the water.

Clyde yelled for help, put the camera down and ran toward Wes. Instantly both Mike and Andy jumped into rescue mode. Andy jumped up to run and within a few strides ripped a calf muscle in his leg and couldn't move another step. Mike ran on without his brother, out into the water and tried to rouse Wes. Clyde was right beside Mike, and together, they assessed Wes' condition. It was clear that Wes needed to be pulled from the water. Mike lifted Wes and began to drag him back toward shore. About that time, another huge wave crashed over the two of them, and the water washed away Mike's prescription glasses and his iPhone.

Mike dragged Wes to the shore. Wes was bleeding and unable to catch his breath. A big wave had smashed him into the ocean floor and he was in extreme pain and very disoriented. A fireman who was in the wedding party checked out Wes' injuries. Wes had a cut over his eye from hitting the ocean floor and severe pain in his neck. Carolyn wrapped a towel around Wes, and he tried to walk it off. Aside from Andy's torn muscle and Mike's soaked iPhone and missing glasses, everything seemed to be okay. Wes and Carolyn decided to skip the wedding and just go on to Utah where they had a vacation home. As Wes and Carolyn left the beach, I limped along the shoreline, looking for Mike's glasses, so grateful for how the crisis had turned out.

The next day, Andy and I had matching gaits. I was still limping from my throbbing knee, and Andy limped as he walked Andrea down the aisle for a beautiful wedding. But other than that, everything went as Cathy had planned. Our family enjoyed a wonderful time celebrating, and all too soon it was time for all of us go home. That's when we found out that Wes had sought medical help in Utah where it was determined that he had broken his neck in three places! What a miracle that Wes hadn't been paralyzed while traveling.

Clyde called Wes at his rehab facility to comfort and encourage him. We were so grateful that Wes was expected to fully recover and stunned at the many risks of paralysis or even death that could have happened to Wes when he was walking around and traveling to Utah with a broken neck. Wes' doctors were amazed that, despite the seriousness of the injuries and the lack of proper care to prevent further injury, Wes was expected to fully recover. Clyde chuckled as he chatted with Wes, noting that despite the seriousness of the injury and the pain, Wes still had his fabulous sense of humor.

"When I took that wave," Wes said to Clyde. "I didn't realize it would take me in at break-neck speed."

The weekend wound up with all our family happily exhausted as Andrea and her husband, Kelly, left for a Hawaiian honeymoon. My knee continued to ache, but the joy of each moment clouded the pain. I thought the drama of the weekend was over, when I learned that Miguel, a member of the wedding party, had performed emergency care for a transient who had stumbled into an elegant restaurant the day after the wedding. The transient had been stabbed and came into the restaurant profusely bleeding and seeking help. Miguel responded immediately, jumped up and stuffed several napkins into the man's bleeding chest then performed CPR when the man went into cardiac arrest. Because of the transient's lifestyle, Miguel would have to undergo treatment and testing for HIV, all because of his Good Samaritan reaction.

Clyde pushed me in a wheelchair down the airport concourse for our trip home. I finally conceded that I needed some help managing my knee discomfort, and Clyde was more than willing to accommodate me. As I listened to the hum of the jet engines on my return flight, I chuckled as I thought of the assortment of plans and actual events of the weekend. I thought about how God had provided Andrea with such a beautiful wedding and how much I enjoyed being with family to celebrate.

I also thought about all the plans that were interrupted that weekend with so many strange things like a power failure, a surfing rescue, a wrenched knee and a torn calf muscle. I admired how calmly Cathy solved problems, using her tenacity, imagination, resources and resolve. I pondered how Andy, so dedicated to his mission of safety for his city, yet also devoted to his family, balanced the two commitments in the midst of chaos.

I could see where God had been present throughout all the weekend plans, pains and interruptions. Even when I returned home I could see God providing for our family through those events. I received a phone call from my son Mike, on his brand new IPhone. When Mike went to replace his iPhone, the company heard his story of the rescue and offered to give him a new phone at no charge. That prompted me to pray for a similar end to the story of Mike's missing prescription glasses that are still floating around the Pacific Ocean. Sure enough, a few days later, Wes and Carolyn replaced Mike's glasses.

I think God put me in the midst of all those plans and interruptions to teach me that, while it's prudent to plan, I need to be ready to lean on Him if he allows interruptions. And maybe He's also trying to teach me that when the next wedding arrives, I either need to be more careful with my exercise routine or simply buy a dress in a bigger size.

SNAPSHOT 36

The Family Legacy

Clyde and I have been blessed to work with our children in ministry on many levels. Now that we are retired, we live within 20 miles of both Tim and Lori. We interact with their ministries on a regular basis in person. Clyde and I support Mike's ministry in New England and Andy's on-line blog ministry for police officers in San Diego from afar. Sunday nights are our family debriefing sessions, where we gather either in person, or via telephone or Skype to compare notes and gain wisdom about the various ministries we are all working on. We celebrate victories and offer encouragement and suggestions for problems. Our children and their spouses know each other so well, that they can offer insights into solutions quickly, capitalizing on the talents and tendencies each of them possesses. We all know who God has created each of us to be, and we try to use that knowledge for God's purposes.

My son, Tim, is the youngest in our family and the most like me of all the children. Tim is lively, out-going, challenge-driven and full of chutzpah. Tim's ministry has ranged from serving as a youth pastor to senior pastor to church plant administrator. He has always capitalized on his natural God-given talents and the role modeling in his life. When Tim married Michelle, she was only 18 and thrust into the role of a pastor's wife. Michelle had so many wonderful qualities that made her perfect for this job; she just didn't know it Yet.

Tim:

One of Mom's gifts has always been to see an opening or willingness in someone and not waste time with it. I saw that growing up all the time. If Mom saw a heart softening, she dropped everything to respond. In the beginning of our marriage, Michelle was excited to see where God might take us with our ministry. Mom saw a scared openness in Michelle and immediately started working with it. Mom didn't see inexperience or a young faith; Mom saw possibilities.

Mom inspired a love for the lost within Michelle and Michelle has never strayed from that vision. Michelle and Mom believe that everyone has a need to know the Lord, even if they don't know it. Mom is also a firm believer that you have to be who you really are. As Mom mentored Michelle she insisted that Michelle had to be who God had created her to be, not what the congregation thought she should be. The result was that Michelle never lost her love for ministry. The pastor's wife reflects the personality of the church. Michelle is fun, always smiling and dresses fashionably, just like Mom. I've had people tell me that they came to our church the first time simply because of Michelle's style. That's God working through Michelle the way He created her.

The Sunday night sessions with the family are my best means of counsel. Mom and Dad have a lifetime of experience to draw from. I know that I will receive honest feedback from everyone, and they won't always agree with my point of view. It's also comforting to know that Dad is firm when he believes that I'm right and encourages me to stand up for my conviction on an issue. Each week I am encouraged to see how anger or defensiveness disappears with honest, respectful perspective from my sister, mother, father, brother-in-law or brothers. Even if they disagree with me, their comments and ideas are cloaked in love. Dad has the gavel. When Dad feels something passionately, he's firm. And he is brutally honest.

Mom is the eternal encourager. She always sees the possibilities within the challenge, and she's excited to see how God will work within the problem. Mom often reminds us to be who God created us to be despite the stress. It's comforting and inspiring for each of us to have affirmation to honor God with our personalities as well as our ministries.

My oldest son, Mike, is a pastor in New England. He began his church as a "church plant," meaning that there was no church at all, and Mike and his wife, Ellen, invited people into their home to learn about God, and a church grew from there. Church planting is probably the most challenging forms of ministry, but it is also often the most rewarding. Mike was called to ministry as a teenager and he practices a powerful method of sharing Jesus wherever he goes.

Mike:

From Israel to Russia and from the east coast to west coast here in America, people who encounter Gerrie soon realize there is something special about this woman. Those of us who are closest to her know that what sets Mom apart is her deeply grounded faith.

Mom's faith is not just "who" she is with this God-given charismatic personality and natural beauty, but in "whose" she is. Mom is God's ambassador who truly loves people and they love her in return as she leads them right to Yashua (the original Hebrew or Aramaic name of Jesus).

As a result, living out her faith not just in the public eye but at home with family behind the scenes, my mother has made a lasting impact not only on me but on my wife, Ellen. The example of my mother and my father's strong, uncompromising faith in Christ has resulted in Ellen and I having the courage to personally take such big risks and steps of faith that only God could make happen. It was with faith that Ellen and I endeavored to start a church in New England, the most un-churched region of the country. We have witnessed how time after time God has answered my mother's prayers of faith. Through Mom's example and encouragement, I know that if I am in the center of God's perfect will, He will answer my prayers in faith.

Ellen – Mike's Wife:

Being married to Gerrie's oldest son, Mike, I have had the privilege for 31 years to observe my dear mother-in-law as a wife, mother, and pastor's wife and close friend. Gerrie's strong faith has helped her balance all these areas of life with grace and she has been a tremendous role model and mentor. I truly feel blessed to have her in my life. She is a woman of faith.

My son, Andy, was recently appointed to Captain of the San Diego Police Department. His career life is very different from the other children, yet Andy works in ministry through his work just the same. Andy writes weekly blogs called "Devotions 4 Cops" with readers around the world. Andy's target audience is law enforcement personnel, and the purpose of the blog is to encourage cops in their faith. But his message is often timely and poignant for anyone. http://www.devotions4cops.com.

Andy:

I have a photo of me on the sidelines of a Taylor University football game. I had just come out of the game and was getting a drink while the defense was on the field. I heard someone calling my name in a sweet feminine voice. It was my mom.

"Sweetie, that was a pretty hard hit, did it hurt much?" Mom asked. "Are you okay?"

Talking out of the side of my mouth I answered her, "Mom, you can't be on the field."

It didn't matter to Mom. She always wanted to be involved, in the game, at the vortex of life.

This continued into my professional life as a cop. Let me explain first that cell phones are both a blessing and a curse. I always carry mine; it's part of the job. But one day, I seriously considered rethinking that habit. During a quasi SWAT mission, my team of men had a guy barricaded in a house. He was armed and dangerous and wanted for a few robberies. It was our mission to get the guy out safely, hopefully without killing him or getting one of my guys hurt.

Tactically, men were positioned around the house using cover and concealment. I whispered into the radio being piped into their ear pieces, "Mission update. Suspect One is still inside and we are ready to initiate a contain and call-out. Any intelligence our updates..." Suddenly I was interrupted with RING! RING! RING! My cell phone went off.

"Standby." I reported to my men. I figured it was a Chief Officer asking for an update or the SWAT Commanding Officer wanting to know if we needed their equipment and resources.

No, it was my mother. "Hi honey. I'm just calling to see how you are doing."

I swallowed and replied as quietly as I could, "Mom, now is not a good time." I looked to my right and three of my sergeants were laughing hysterically.

"Why?" Mom persisted. "What's going on?"

"It's kind of hard to explain right now, Mom," I replied as kindly as a son could answer and still maintain my professional protocol. "But I'll call you later." I disconnected the call to re-focus on the job at hand. People's lives depended on it.

The police radio was crackling in the background when my cell phone rang again. I hit the button immediately. "Mom?"

"No," A deep masculine voice replied. It was the Chief. "I hear you have a mission. Can you give me an update?

I sighed. "Sure...it's a long story."

Mom likes to be at the center of all that's going on, small issues or large events. She wants to be in and on the front line. It is true of her faith, her passions, her family and her church. She is so vivacious it reminds me of the scripture from Zachariah 8:23, which I have paraphrased, "Their faith was so real that ten people latched onto one Jew and said we hear you know God." That is Mom's faith and her legacy.

Cathy – Andy's Wife

Gerrie is awesome at making you feel like whatever you're doing is the greatest thing in the world. She is always warm and fun and friendly. What really stands out for me is that whenever we are together, no matter how much time has passed since our last visit, it seems like yesterday. There are never any awkward moments with Gerrie. She is a person of unconditional love.

My daughter, Lori, and I enjoy a rich, fun, best friend relationship. Lori is successful in business but has also been a pastor's wife for many years.

Lori:

All my life I've had friends say, "Lori, I so wish I could be a part of your family." The joy between my mom and dad and their love for the Lord not only spilled over to me, but also to my friends. A lot of pastor's kids struggle with being the "example" for church families (the fish bowl effect), but I actually grew up feeling special and felt that it was actually a privilege to be a Christian and a pastor's kid. I was thrilled that my mom and dad were in ministry. The thing I enjoyed the most was how both Mom and Dad made Christian faith fun, exciting and contemporary. They didn't teach us that living our faith was a list of things we should or shouldn't do, but instead, it was lifestyle of privileges, fun and excitement to see God working in our lives.

Our house was the hub of excitement in the church and community. We lived out in the middle of nowhere, and the church was next door. The door was always open for people to drop by to hang out. They came for card games, Evelyn's popcorn, Mom's endless supply of chocolate chip cookies, root beer floats and just good, old-fashioned fun. When the church built a gym, even more people came to our house, and when I think about it now, I'm not quite sure how Mom kept our house so tidy and orderly with four kids of her own and a whole community of teenagers and sweaty basketball players stomping through without notice. But she was always happy to see everyone who showed up and greeted them warmly with a hug and welcomed them in.

When difficult things happened, Mom and Dad taught us how to embrace those challenges rather than just endure them. They taught us how to turn to the Bible and search to find scriptures that were fitting for the situation we were in. We would often stop and pray about our questions and dilemmas and wait together to see just how God was going to provide a solution. They taught us that faith was such a comfort and joy, and our daily discoveries were all part of the exciting adventures of the Christian life. What a gift. And they practiced what they preached.

I still have a vision of my parents in my head that I witnessed as a teenager one night. It was well past midnight and something woke me. The door to my room was open and across the hall I could see the silhouettes of Mom and Dad kneeling at their bed and praying together. I held my breath as I could hear Dad quietly praying and Mom crying softly. He said, "Lord, please help us to love those who are hurting us. Though their claws are out and our backs are raw, please help us to work through this and love them the way you want us to. Help us to become stronger and better in all this, and may we bring honor and glory to you by responding and not reacting."

That example of love in the face of their deep hurt has stayed with me throughout my entire life. At the time, I didn't even know Mom and Dad were going through anything; they were so cautious about sharing these types of things with their children. But seeing their pain and hearing their solution that night so long ago was beautiful and such a great example for me, a teenager with my own struggles, that quite honestly paled in comparison. This brief moment in time became a strong and guiding light for me throughout my entire life and in my own ministry, many times over.

No one on earth has a greater appreciation for the little ways that God blesses others than my mom. Every time I talk with Mom she has a list of things to share that God has done for her. "I have a blessing to share with you," is how she usually starts out on most of our phone calls. Or, "Just wait until we get together. I have something huge to tell you; but this one has to wait until I am looking into the whites of your eyes. You are going to be just thrilled to hear how God has blessed..." Mom celebrates God in such an extreme way, and it continually rubs off on everyone around her. Her enthusiasm and sensitivity to how God interacts in her daily life helps all of us around her to see the things He's doing in our own lives as well.

Mom has always been my best friend growing up and such a delight in my life. I just adore her. She was the matron of honor in my wedding, and we are still best buds. We love shopping together, chatting on the phone and just sitting down for a mid afternoon cup of decaf coffee to share our latest developments, big and small. It's amazing to me how similar our taste is.

Several years ago, when I was living in Canada, my husband graciously offered me the opportunity to visit Mom and Dad in Florida because I hadn't seen them in awhile. When I got off the plane Mom and I couldn't help but laugh as we went to hug one another for we were both carrying the exact, same purse. We lived thousands of miles away from each other, with millions of handbags to choose from between us, and yet somehow, someway, we managed to select the same exact purse and the same exact color. Imagine that!

Mom is also our family's greatest cheerleader. No matter what we do, any endeavor, personally or professionally, she is in the front row cheering us on. It was a real shock when my siblings and I all came to the realization that we weren't the smartest, fastest and best. (But Mom doesn't know that yet. Please don't burst her bubble and tell her.)

For many years my husband and I lived thousands of miles away from our families because our ministry required it. Today, our ministry has led us to live close enough to Mom and Dad and my brother Tim's family that we can get together several times a week if we want to for coffee, lunch or shopping. This is such a treat.

One thing Mom and I do not share in common is that I love camping and her idea of camping is staying in a hotel without room service. When Mom and Dad came to visit us in Canada, it was a 10 hour drive from the airport to our home. On one of their visits we agreed that we needed to spend the night en route; however, the cost of hotels just didn't fit our budget. So after chatting with Dad, my husband Mark and I decided to surprise Mom with her first camping experience. Mark and I set up the tent at a local KOA in Northern Maine, and then drove on to the airport to pick Mom and Dad up. When Mom walked off the plane, I knew we were in for quite an experience. She looked like a million bucks in her pink sateen suit, sparkling diamonds and high heels – her typical Hollywood style. Dad's grin and wink put me at ease, but I fought the giggles when Mom asked if we had the reservations all taken care of for the hotel. I swiftly explained that we had great accommodations and that we were thrilled with them. I could only imagine what was coming.

After driving several hours, we reached our destination. "A KOA campground?" she exclaimed. "Is this a joke? I am not staying here! I am NOT a camper."

But in this remote part of Maine there were no other options, so with some encouragement from Mark and me about how fun camping was and Dad's firm stand, Mom bedded down next to

Dad in a sleeping bag, expressing her deepest sentiments, "How could you be my daughter, Lori?"

Mark, Dad and I fell asleep laughing.

During the night it began to rain, and Mom needed to go to the bathroom. I got the flashlight and walked with her to the bathroom across the campground. She looked adorable in her long white robe with the ruffle around the bottom and her feathery mule slippers with the clear plastic heels. Seeing her schlep through the mud puddles to and from the tent was a sight I will never forget. The next morning Mom and Dad stood under an umbrella together in the downpour while Mark and I cheerfully packed up the tent, having a total blast.

Mom huddled up to Dad, trying to stay dry and warm. She gripped the umbrella handle and began questioning again, "Lori, how could you be my daughter? What has Mark done to you? How in the world can you call this fun?"

The truth is, all in all, Mom is a great sport most of the time. Even when she is out of her comfort zone she tries hard to be optimistic and upbeat and exercise true faith, especially when we gently remind her that she is to be our example. (We love to pull that line on her once in a while. It works!) And the best part is how real and humble she is when she realizes some adjustments need to be made. She has shown me time and time again, from my earliest recollections, how important it is to just roll with the punches, stay close to God, leave it all in his hands, and make adjustments when needed.

For this I am so grateful; because for me, raising three boys while working as an account executive, trying hard to be a diligent pastor's wife and everything in between required a lot of deep faith and rolling with the punches. Mom's example has been a true blessing for me to follow and wouldn't you know it, I now get those gentle little reminders from my kids too. Oy Vey! The legacy lives on.

Mark – Lori's Husband:

We have all heard it said that the "acorn does not fall from the tree." If a son has a sense of humor like his father and tells a joke at a party, someone in the room will laughingly blurt out their "acorn" statement. When a child exhibits a bad temper, murmurs are whispered, "Looks like the acorn sure doesn't fall far from that tree." How true this anecdote seems to be in our day-to-day experiences of watching learned behavior, which has been passed down from parents to their children.

I will never forget pulling up to the parsonage of the church at five minutes to midnight, July 2nd and walking into Lori's home. The room was still filled with family and friends from the church. What would make so many adults stay up so late? It was obvious that, like me, they deeply admired Lori, and wanted to see what kind of "acorn" she was bringing home to meet THE FOLKS (or shall say, the oaks?). But it was more than that. What I experienced that night was the beginning of years of observation of some of the greatest people I have ever known, the oaks in Lori's life. I saw exactly where the girl of my dreams had developed such inner and outer grace and beauty, such attractiveness. "The acorn had simply not fallen far from the tree!"

I have had ample time over the years to examine the oaks in Lori's life. I, too, have set myself about the task of learning and emulating the behavior of these well-planted, godly parents of my spouse. There is so much to admire about my father-in-law, Clyde Mills, as the Mighty Oak of the Mills clan and my mother-in-law, Gerrie, who inspires everyone. The two of them purposefully and carefully crafted the lives of my wife, and her three brothers. Those children stand today as her legacy.

It's been said, "Be careful who you marry. Like mother, like daughter." After personally knowing and loving the mother of my wife, this oak named Gerrie Hyman Mills, I say, I am so glad I did, because the acorn does not fall far from the tree!

My grandchildren are very dear to me and I have enjoyed watching them grow up. But when I thought about special memories to share with my readers, there were so many, I didn't know where to start. So instead, I've invited my grandchildren to share their memories in their own words.

From the Mouths of my grand babes

Jonathan:

I can remember my whole life, from when I was a child until recently, how Grandma would come storming through our front door like Yenta in the musical "Fiddler on the Roof" to tell my mom her big news. "Lori, you wouldn't BELIEVE my blessing today," Grandma would exclaim. "I got an extra 30% off on paintbrushes at Michaels..."

I have always admired how Grandma is appreciative of every tiny little blessing that God gives her day to day. She thanks the Lord for her favorite flowers that decorate her front porch, her samples of the day at See's Candy, and for the most special of times we have all been able to spend together.

As I have been growing up and becoming an adult, I notice how Grandma's mustard seed faith blesses me every day. I have learned to be grateful for the smallest of things and to live life to the fullest. Grandma won't let circumstances get her down. When the challenges of life come at her full force, she prays hard; and instead of being upset and depressed, it's a matter of hours before you find her planning a party, painting candles and vases, and heading over to the mall to get chocolate. I love how you can't keep Grandma down, and that is why she is such a strong woman of God. I am so glad to have both Grandma and Grandpa in my life to show me an example of not only living a life revolving around Jesus, but celebrating that kind of life.

Nathan:

When my mom (Lori Mills Welch) was a little girl, Grandma taught Mom to pray daily for her future husband. Night after night Mom would pray that whoever and wherever he was, that the Lord would protect him and keep him pure for her. The Lord brought my dad into Mom's life, and there is no doubt that God brought the two of them together and answered my mom's prayer.

When I was five years old my mom passed Grandma's "future spouse prayer" on to me, and I learned to pray that prayer every night before bed. As I got older I added a few specific requests to that prayer as well. We will keep some of those between me and God. But what I can say is that on August 19, 2006, I married the girl of my dreams, the girl I had been praying for.

Grandma passed on such an incredible legacy to us and to many other families, and I am so blessed to be her grandchild. Before my wife and I were officially dating, I remember saying to Grandma before anyone else, "You know what, Grandma? I'm going to marry that girl."

Well Grandma, thanks for your extra prayers, because I reeled her in!

David:

My grandmother's faith is anything but boring. She has always integrated fun into faith. We were never afraid of it. She taught us that faith is exciting, faith is real, and faith is celebrating blessings, no matter the size.

Grandma has always been original, and has constantly found fun and creative ways of making others enjoy life to the fullest. As children, she would allow us to mix colored mini-marshmallows into our macaroni and then would hold our hands as we thank God for the "nourishing food" we were eating.

We have been blessed to be together in Israel three times, and I will never forget her surprising everyone on the trip by dressing up as the "woman at the well" and giving a monologue about how Jesus saved her. She may have been acting, but for me, she genuinely brought a tangible image of what a faith-filled woman of the Bible would have been like. In America, she is the only Jewish believer many Christians have ever interacted with. For most Christians, the Jewish world is completely foreign to them, even though it is the root of their faith. Grandma helps people reconnect with the Jewish personality of faith in Jesus.

Even though there have been several periods of time when we have lived far away from each other, Grandma and Grandpa have made a concerted effort to be a part of our lives. The ways in which they have plugged-in and invested in their grandchildren reminds me of how God meets us where we are and loves us for who we are. Even when I was studying 2,000 miles away, Grandma purchased a plane ticket to come see me in my plays. She even found a way to visit me in my apartment in Israel. She works hard to be a good grandmother to all of her grandchildren, whether it is painting with Caroline, making mud pies with Wil, cheering for Reed at his races or Rachel in her surfing competitions, whether she is baking a cake that looked like the beach with Alexa, or meeting Steffenie and Andrea at the trendiest new restaurant or Gemma, Aubrie and Aundrea at See's candy in the mall, or going to Nathan's rock concerts (even though she does not always like his genre of music), or reposting Jonathan's latest acting adventure on her Facebook wall. As all of us were growing up, she reflected God's character of loving differences and encouraged each one of us to be individuals and to follow our dreams.

I have never known Grandma to be one for keeping things to herself, especially when those things are blessings. After she receives blessings, she tells everybody (and I mean everyone) about them. I believe that is part of the reason why God likes blessing her, because He gets a kick out of watching her tell everyone about it!

I suppose being so involved and attached to me made it harder than usual for her to see me move to Israel and develop a life for myself there. I think the hardest part was probably me swearing into the military of a country that has seen its fair share of wars. Grandpa was proud of me, and Grandma was begging me not to do it, but eventually she supported me and knew that I was doing what I believe God wanted from me. They and my parents instilled in me at a young age that, as long as I was praying, and in God's will, that they would support my decisions.

Grandma has been infected with a matchmaking gene and from time to time she used it on me, even when it was uncomfortable. When I was dating Gemma, she approached me and said, "This is just bothering me. I don't know if you're going to be really upset with me or not, but I have to speak my piece. I don't picture you and Gemma together. I picture her with somebody more like your brother Nathan."

At the time I was shocked, but of course kept it to myself. I realized just how good Grandma's matchmaking senses were, however, when my brother Nathan and Gemma were married.

Once when Grandma came to visit me at my university in Indiana, she had scoped out the whole university. She asked me, "David, are any of the girls here catching your eye?"

I blushingly asked her why she was asking.

She continued, "Well, I have one picked out for you."

After asking her which girl that was, I realized from her detailed description that the girl was none other than the one I had been secretly interested in for months! I never doubted her senses after that.

Aubrie:

When my mom and dad left Michigan and moved to California, I entered fifth grade. California was so different from my home in Michigan; we might as well have moved to the moon. I had very little in common with these kids in our new upscale Northern California community, who had swimming pools, designer clothes and a materialistic philosophy. I had a very hard time fitting in. I had a funny Midwestern accent, very different clothes, and a strong faith that resulted in being teased and tormented at school. I was even stabbed in the back with a pencil. It was a huge test of faith, trying to be kind to kids who were so cruel to me. In seventh grade a classmate, who epitomized the "mean girl" concept, created a petition on poster board for other students to sign, agreeing not to be friends with me. It was hard to live the life of love and forgiveness when she gathered signatures from about 600 students and forged signatures of anyone who wouldn't sign her poster.

Grandma was concerned about me, and she began a family prayer vigil for me to make just one good friend. Middle school had been brutal, and I felt so isolated and unloved at school. When I entered high school, it seemed like the whole family was praying for me to find just one good, solid, stable, Christian friend. Whenever I saw Grandma, she reminded me that she, Grandpa, my Aunt Lori and all her boys were praying for me to find one good friend at my new high school.

My cousin, David, had just graduated from my high school, and he knew a Christian girl my age named Halley. David said he would try to arrange for Halley and me to meet when school started. My new high school had nearly 3000 students, and I was nervous enough just trying to find my classes. I wasn't looking for an awkward introduction through David to compound my first day jitters.

On my very first day of high school, I had dance class first block. A petite girl with long dark hair came up to me after roll call and said, "Are you David Mills' cousin?"

I nodded, then braced myself for a trick or threat or some kind of unpleasantness to follow, but instead she said, "Hi, I'm Halley. David told me about you. Let's get in the same warm-up group." And ever since that day, 10 years ago, Halley and I have been close friends. Even when I moved to a different high school, Halley and I remained friends. Grandma's fervent prayers were answered beyond my wildest hope, for not only does Halley share my Christian values, she and I have personalities that click, and we will be friends forever.

While I was in high school, I fell in love with a boy who challenged me on many levels. My mom and dad were so unhappy about my relationship with this boy, but I could always talk to Grandma about him. Unlike Mom and Dad, Grandma didn't lecture me, but I knew what she was thinking. Yet her counsel was always asking me what I wanted from the relationship; not telling me what I should be getting. But the one thing I knew about Grandma was that she didn't just listen, she prayed, always believing that God would speak to my heart. But as I began to make inappropriate choices with this boyfriend, my entire extended family became concerned as the lies caught up with me.

One day Mom, Grandma and I met my Uncle Mike in Florida for a brief visit. Uncle Mike and I are very close, and I have always adored him. He dropped Mom and Grandma off and asked me to go with him to Target to pick up a few items.

"You can wait here," Uncle Mike said, turning up the stereo, as he parked the car. "I'll be right back."

So I waited in the car remembering all the fun Uncle Mike and I always had whenever we would get together. I could hardly wait to see what he had planned for us this afternoon. A new movie, an amusement park, a water slide, whatever; I was ready. Uncle Mike and I always had fun together.

Very soon, Uncle Mike returned to the car with a small Target shopping bag. He got in the car, but he didn't start the engine, instead he turned down the music and rolled down the window.

"So Aubrie, tell me about school. How are things going? Are you still dating that guy?"

"Yep," I nodded, watching Uncle Mike open the Target bag and take out a carpenter's tape measure. "But we've kind of hit a rough patch," I admitted, "I found out he was cheating on me with another girl."

"Well, do you think you deserve that kind of treatment?" Uncle Mike asked.

"No," I told him. "But he's a good guy at heart," I was good at rationalizing and making excuses for my boyfriend.

"Does this guy weaken your relationship with God?" Uncle Mike asked.

I gulped. "I don't know," I replied. "I don't think so. I still have my faith."

"But it sounds like you've been telling a lot of lies to be with him," Uncle Mike said directly. "Do you think that pleases God?"

I stared at Uncle Mike, as he unwrapped the tape measure from the plastic wrapper and began to push the end of the tape out the window of the car. Even though I could always confide in Uncle Mike, his questions were making me uncomfortable.

"I don't know," I admitted. "I hadn't really thought about it that way."

Uncle Mike kept pushing the tape out into the Target parking lot, farther and farther. I could see the end of the tape scraping the pavement. First it was out about 20 feet out, then 30, then 50, and he kept pushing the tape farther as cars swerved around it, and shoppers pushed carts over it.

"Aubrie, can you see the end of the tape from here?" Uncle Mike asked me as the 100 foot tape was completely pushed out of the case and into the parking lot. "Can you see the one inch marker?"

"Not really," I said. "It's kind of a long way out there." I thought Uncle Mike had lost his mind, pushing a perfectly good tape measure out into the parking lot to be run over by cars and distracting drivers.

"That once inch mark is the part of your life timeline that you are focusing on right now, Aubrie. Think of this tape measure as your whole lifetime and that one inch mark, way out there, is what you are thinking about today."

"Okay," I said doubtfully, wondering what he was trying to teach me.

"Aubrie," Uncle Mike continued looking directly at me. "The part of the tape between that one inch mark and right here at the 100 foot mark is your life. Try to think of those 100 feet as the future that God has for you. See how long and far it is?"

I nodded.

"Aubrie, God has a future for you that doesn't include lying to your parents or being mistreated or disrespected by a boyfriend. But you get to choose. What kind of future do you want?"

"I want to be loved and happy," I told him.

"The decisions you're making now are going to affect your future of both love and happiness," Uncle Mike said. "You need *to decide if this is the route you want to take with your life. Just look at how long that lifeline is!"*

Uncle Mike began to reel in the tape measure, and I sat there stunned. His tape measure object lesson really put my situation in a whole different perspective, and I knew in my heart what I had to do. It took me awhile to gather to courage to sever my relationship with my boyfriend, but I did it, and today I look back on that conversation in the Target parking lot as one of the most important moments of my life.

What I didn't know was that Mom and Grandma were praying for me and Uncle Mike that day. They knew how much I admired, respected and adored Uncle Mike and that I might be able to hear the truth from him better than from the others who loved me. Grandma's faith was honored as God spoke to my heart through Uncle Mike's object lesson in a way that I will always remember. In fact, I still have the tape measure!

Aundrea:

Grandma is a woman of action. She is quick to respond to any crisis, need or situation where she can help. No matter what, I can count on my grandma to help me use my faith to solve problems or ease uncomfortable situations.

When I broke up with a boy I had been dating for two years, it was heartbreaking. I really cared for my boyfriend, but I also knew that he was growing in a different direction and not the same as me.

When Grandma found out about the breakup, she rushed over to my house to bring me flowers and a sweet card. Her love and concern surrounded me in a way that no one else could. I grew up knowing about Grandma's love story, and I knew that she understood the depth of a high school crush. But Grandma didn't just let me wallow in grief; she reminded me to think positively about my future without this boy I loved, and to praise God for all the plans God had ahead for me.

Grandma was right. My heart mended and I was able to move on into a bright future. Grandma also encouraged me to pray for God's direction in my life the same as she does in hers. Grandma is always so genuine and sincere when she shares her faith with me. And she uses that Jewish chutzpah to tell me things that touch my heart. I know Grandma will always give me advice to help my relationship with God, and faith will sustain me when I hit those bumps in the road.

SNAPSHOT 37

My Jewish Roots Run Deep

My life as a child was immersed in Jewish culture. Even as I grew into my teens and began to make friends on my own, I didn't socialize much outside of the Jewish community. Friday nights after synagogue services were overflowing with fun, and back then it was unimaginable that I would not be part of this fun for my entire life. Celebrating holidays or family events were especially enjoyable within my Jewish family, and I looked forward to Jewish weddings or the Jewish High Holy Days with eager anticipation. But, for all of my formative years, being Jewish had nothing to do with God or religion; being Jewish was simply a rich culture and an enchanting social world.

How could I marry outside of my faith? I have no doubt in my mind that it was God's plan for me. When I invited Jesus into my life, I didn't join a new religion; I began a relationship with

God. Facing the disappointment, anger and devastation of my parents, sister, cousins, grandparents, aunts and uncles was the hardest thing I ever had to do. I loved my family with the same fervor and passion that they loved me and I never wanted to hurt them. But I could not deny my new-found faith and my love for Jesus.

I tried to explain my Christian faith to my father, but he could not comprehend it. When I told Daddy that Jesus had saved me he shouted, "You get yourself unsaved." Those words of rage deeply hurt me. I loved Daddy with all my heart, but his anger and disappointment were nothing compared to the sadness I felt at his lack of understanding. As intensely as I loved Daddy, and as much as I wanted to be obedient to his wishes, I gathered my courage and waved good bye.

I didn't want to be ostracized from the family, yet I knew that I could never give up what I had found with the Lord. God had given me a strong sense of fulfillment in my life; it was something I had been longing for. Before I began my relationship with God, I was just existing without a purpose. When I accepted the Lord in my life, something swelled inside of me, and I felt a happiness that I'd never experienced before. I prayed for God to help me through my family's outrage, and I was so eager to be His child and to keep that happy contentment that nothing my family could say would dissuade me.

Before I knew God, my confidence was all built around having a lot of friends, parties, events, and family; that was my security. And that's why I felt so empty all the time, because whenever one of those events ended, I found myself for looking for more. Once Jesus came into my life, I was no longer looking for something to fill that void. This newness of life was centered on God Himself.

It was difficult to hold my ground in the beginning of my walk with God. I had been surrounded all my life by this wonderful, loving, consuming Jewish family. When I became a Christian, to them it appeared that I was abandoning all they had invested in me. They had watched me grow up, and to many of them I was the daring darling of the clan, the blonde sparkler who always had spunk and style. They felt betrayed when I chose Clyde, but when they realized that I had embraced the Christian faith, they were devastated. It took divine guidance from God and enormous courage for me to refuse to deny my faith.

Eventually, my family accepted Clyde as my husband, Christianity as my faith and ministry as my career. But it was a long process and being accepted is not the same as being approved of. I'm sure I will always remain a bit of a black sheep among the family memoires, and I deeply regret the hurt that I caused my family.

I carry a note from my father in my Bible. It arrived shortly after I told him that Clyde was giving up his business career to go to Bible college. I think of it as an olive branch from Daddy. God had softened his heart to see God at work in our lives. The note reads:

Dearest children, Just a line to say all is okay at home. A bit bewildered about it all but I can assure you are not confused. I'm at a loss to know how you two will be able to accomplish so much in so little time. Naturally your one big obstacle is your debt to the credit union. But you both seem so positive that you can mount it. Time will tell. If Clyde is accepted, I am positive that he will make the grade. All my love to you dear, the children and Clyde – Dad

This note was Daddy's way of accepting me, my faith and my calling. I knew that he still didn't like it, but he loved me despite it and believed that Clyde and I would be successful. The note arrived just as Clyde and I were about to embark on the trip to Bible college. It was the best gift from God I could have received.

Time did tell, and while Daddy and I didn't discuss all the details, I know that he could see that God was there to help Clyde and I pay our bills, follow through with our responsibilities and provide for Bible college expenses. Daddy's kind note made me aware that his heart was tender enough to see God at work. I have raised my children to cherish their Jewish heritage. Like my parents reminded me, I have taught them to be proud of being Jewish. We are a very close-knit family, interacting with each other almost daily. All four of my children are involved in Christian ministry in one way or another, and they are all committed to fulfilling God's purposes in their lives. They, in turn, are teaching the same values to my grandchildren.

I have a great love for the Jewish community. I think of them as "my people," and I enjoy socializing and celebrating Jewish traditions. I share my Christian faith with my Jewish friends when I can, but it's not contingent on my friendship with anyone Jewish.

Jewish people have been called "The Chosen People," based on the Old Testament teachings in the Bible. God has a special love for those who were born Jewish. But Jewish people who desire to have life after death in Heaven with God must come to the Lord the same as everyone.

All who desire a relationship with God must recognize a need for forgiveness and desire peace with God. In return, God promises eternal life. Anyone of any ethnicity, religion or nationality can invite Jesus into their hearts to be their Lord. For Jewish people, this is called becoming a Messianic Jew; still embracing the Jewish faith, but including the love and forgiveness of Jesus, the promised Messiah.

I believe that Jesus is a living, breathing person who died but rose from the grave. All we have to do is receive Jesus into our hearts and into our lives, and we will have a relationship with God. It's not a religion; it's a relationship.

I could not complete this book without offering my readers an opportunity to accept Jesus into their hearts. If you desire to know God and have a relationship with Him, ask Him with a simple prayer.

Mike & Ellen

Tim & Michelle

Andy & Cathy

Mark & Lori

The Mills
Andy, Lori, Clyde, Gerrie, Tim & Mike

Vintage Hyman
Family Photos

Mike, Andy, Lori & Tim

Roy & Lettie Mills
Clyde's Parents

Tim & Lori

The Family in Israel

Do I know Gerrie? How is 58 years of knowing Gerrie? Being her husband, I feel so fortunate and couldn't love and appreciate her any more than I do.

We click but haven't always. There were times when we clacked, whatever that is, but we do now and have ever since our first four rocky years of marriage when I decided to get my life right with God. Every marriage needs God in it and then they too can experience the happiness that Gerrie and I and countless other believers have.

Our marriage has been so much of God. Because we are opposites, people thought, they will never make it. Wrong! We have found that we like it that way. I am more laid back, far less talkative and at times shy. Gerrie is effervescent, stylish, classy, confident, bold, a wheeler and dealer, loves people and has unlimited friends. Everybody loves Gerrie, there are always a few exceptions, but they are rare.

I smile just thinking of each time Gerrie comes home after being out taking care of business, which always includes Macy's or Nordstroms, always eager to share her day of exciting happenings.

Every day brings new adventures. It may include sharing God with a hurting person, a seeking man or woman, speaking about her first books and now the new one, baking for the lawn men, making chicken soup for a sick friend or getting a special deal. Believe mem, there is never a dull moment with Gerrie.

She has so much love in her heart for others, especially her family. When the children were small, I would tell her you are kissing them too much, you'll smother them. Fortunately, she didn't stop. All of the four them, and their four, adore her.

As a pastor's wife, all of our 50 years of ministry, she wasn't what we would describe as your average pastor's wife. Her loving spirit and her warm personality draws people to her smiling leadership and fun times she provided for church gatherings. She has always been drawn to lasting friendships and leaders who accomplished goals, whether in life itself or in the ministry. Status wasn't ever the criteria; It was showing people the way to the Lord and encouraging them in their new found faith. She has a unique loving way about being a classy (if you don't mind) pastors wife. I love it, because I love her as do our children , their mates and our grandchildren.

All this would have been a sad story with an unhappy ending had we not realized the necessity of receiving Jesus and placing him first in our lives.

My Gerrie is unique, as God has developed this willing woman to become the person he designed her to be.

Gerrie, we've been a match made in heaven.
I love you
Clyde

Dear Jesus,

You've spoken to my heart. I need You in my life and I realize that You died on the cross, rose from the dead to forgive me of my sins. I invite You to come into my life to fill me with Your love. I open the door of my heart, asking You to be my Lord and Savior. Help me to be the kind of person You want me to be. Thank you, Lord for my new beginning.

Amen!

From the Editor (Friend)
By Cynthia Cutts, Developmental Editor

Gerrie Hyman Mills is a Jewish believer who enjoys a powerful relationship with God. Her vivacious personality and deeply grounded faith are effervescent and bubble up through Gerrie as she shares her faith with everyone around her. With a ministry that spans more than 50 years, Gerrie's life has been filled with answered prayer. Her mission each day is to encourage others in faith and to share her blessings. Gerrie is eager to tell how God is working in her life but also takes great delight in pointing out how God works in the lives of those around her.

Gerrie's enthusiasm and pure joy in the Lord are contagious. It's as if Gerrie is surrounded by a divine spiritual energy that swirls around her. Nothing is ever coincidence with Gerrie – it's from God. Nothing is ever happenstance, luck or a twist of fate – it is God working in our lives. Spend a half hour visiting with Gerrie and you will find yourself drawn into a palpable faith that opens your heart to a much clearer view of how vividly God works in the lives of believers.

Holy Chutzpah! is a collection of true stories – snapshots of faith - that demonstrate the faithfulness of God through the every-day life of a Jewish believer. With a traditional Jewish upbringing of common sense values, hard work and proper protocol, Gerrie's acceptance of the Christian faith resulted in the very best of both cultures. Gerrie's Jewish wisdom tempered with her tender Christian heart gives her a keen sense of the depth of love God has for mankind. Woven into Gerrie's experiences is a common theme of a true relationship with God.

Gerrie never misses an opportunity to build a relationship with another person, and by blending her Jewish tendencies with her Christian ones she is highly effective in supporting and encouraging others. Gerrie sees the world with God in it, not only above it, and believes that He is there to be involved in all solutions to life's problems. Gerrie is an active listener which helps people get to the root of trouble, and she is also a creative problem solver. Gerrie is the kind of friend that will take you to exercise class, rather than just tell you that you are getting fat; and she will pray all day that you don't cancel your gym appointment at the last minute or eat that second piece of chocolate cheesecake.

Gerrie has the unique ability to make almost instant connections with people. Her chutzpah gives her courage to say or do things that most of us would never dare. She is ready to dole out her Jewish wisdom or the offer of peace with God without reservation. Her mission field is wherever Gerrie is – on a plane, at the store, in her home or walking the Holy Land; Gerrie is always dialed in to the people around her. She is sincerely eager to ferret out interesting bits of information about others and honestly wants to know about people. Gerrie's interest in others is genuine and her goal remains constant – she wants God to use her for His purpose every day.

I went to the grocery store with Gerrie once to gather a few items to make lunch. As she pushed the shopping cart down the aisles it reminded me of a princess on a float in a parade. Gerrie walked slowly through the store, smiling and waving to all the employees and calling them by name. She had to stop every 20 feet or so to ask personal questions, and within seconds I realized that just like everywhere else I'd been with this incredible woman, the local market was her mission field.

"How's your foot?" Gerrie asked the butcher. "I've been praying for you to heal fast," she told him. "Did your brother find a job yet?" She asked the chef at the deli. "Did you find a place to rent?" She asked the bakery clerk. "I've been praying for your mom," she told the cashier.

It would have taken me five minutes to run into that store, grab a few items to make lunch and check out; but it took Gerrie about an hour. Along the way she insisted that we both sample a new low-fat cheese, sliced roast beef, orange chicken on a toothpick and chocolate dipped cookies. By the time Gerrie walked her mission field and we finished gathering lunch fixings, I wasn't hungry any more. That's how life is with Gerrie – there is usually a destination in her story, but it is the journey that you will remember.

As Gerrie's developmental editor, I've spent countless hours with her, listening (and laughing) to her memories, taking extreme care to keep the integrity of each story. Gerrie is extraordinarily authentic and extremely humble, insisting that all credit and glory for anything in her ministry be solely given to God. Advising us along the way has been Gerrie's husband and Partner in ministry for over 50 years, Pastor Clyde Mills, who has been our fact-checker, confirming the details, dates and authenticity of each chapter. Equally grounded in his faith, Pastor Clyde has shared his observations and admiration for Gerrie's faith. Throughout their life together Clyde has honored Gerrie's ministry and supported her mission goals. A formidable theologian, Pastor Clyde offers an additional perspective on God's presence in Gerrie's ministry, often marveling at Gerrie's innocent faith that sustains her relationship with God.

As you turn the pages of *Holy Chutzpah!* I invite you to hear it through the voice of your new friend, Gerrie, a high fashion, platinum blonde dynamo, who is sort of a combination of Coco Chanel, the Energizer Bunny, Joan of Arc and Goldie Hawn. Imagine Gerrie sitting on her patio in California, nibbling on chocolate bars and sipping her diet Coke, dressed in a classy, bright colored summer outfit, accessorized from the flower in her hair to the rhinestones on her sparkly silver sandals. Hear Gerrie's laughter, her sighs of awe and the depth of passion in her voice as she recalls stories where she knows God was present. You are about to experience a powerful, unique blend of Jewish perspective with a deep Christian faith - and that just might change your life. Holy Chutzpah!

Gerrie Hyman Mills

Appendix A: Picture Identifiers

Snapshot 1: Gerrie boldly assists at a restaurant "Chutzpah in Action"

Snapshot 2: Gerrie & Mark (son-in-law) celebrate God's provision "The Palms"

Snapshot 3: Gerrie's Bar Mitzvah –Gerrie (left) next to sister Bedonna, Father & Mother behind

Snapshot 4: From left to right: Clyde and Gerrie, Gerrie's father, mother, sister Bedonna

Snapshot 5: Clyde & Gerrie's wedding day (Eloped at the Chapel in the Garden, Angola, IN

Snapshot 6: Clyde & Gerrie with family in front of Welston Community Church (First Internship) Top: Gerrie & Clyde, Middle: Andy (left) & Mike, Bottom: Lori & Timmy

Snapshot 7: Oy Vey: – The Negligee

Snapshot 8: Oy Vey! – The picture window

Snapshot 9: Little Timmy (son)

Snapshot 10: The Stackhouse family (Josh, Joey, Lauren & Jeff)

Snapshot 11: The Unexpected visitor

Snapshot 12: Gene VanHoosear and wife Sherry

Snapshot 13: Gerrie the Athlete

Snapshot 14: Back roads...short cut?

Snapshot 15: The miracle delivery

Snapshot 16: "Clyde"... the Great Dane. (Clyde's namesake)

Snapshot 17: Lori (daughter), 1976 homecoming queen, Qunicy High School

Snapshot 18: The music miracle

Snapshot 19: Flight attendant

Snapshot 20: Gerrie, Florida

Snapshot 21: Clyde & Gerrie

Snapshot 22: From left to right: Lynn Turner & Sherry Break (Naples, FL)

Snapshot 23: David (Grandson) with children in Isreal

Snapshot 24: Fizzy Edwards

Snapshot 25: Reggie Walters & Gerrie

Snapshot 26: Anna & Bill Woods

Snapshot 27: Gerrie as :The woman in the well" in Nazareth, Israel

Snapshot 28: Halley Cutts & Aubrie Mills (Grandaughter)

Snapshot 29: Gerrie with Moshka Hivabvand at Costco

Snapshot 30: Gerrie on TV

Snapshot 31: "OY VEY, SUCH A DEAL" Gerrie's first book

Snapshot 32: Gerrie with Patricia Hake

Snapshot 33: Tony & Annie Williams

Snapshot 34: Joe & Barb Riley

Snapshot 35: Clyde with Wes Mills

Snapshot 36: The Family (Love)

Snapshot 37: Gerrie, Larry Rose (cousin), Above: Bob & Bedonna Perish (sister)

Pastor Clyde Mils (My Love)

ABOUT THE AUTHOR

Gerrie lives in Northern California, where she is semi-retired, but still active in supporting the ministries of her children. She is available for keynote speaking at Christian women's retreats, luncheons, workshops and other events. She is also a college lecturer and a veteran tour guide of the Holy Land. She recently began a drama ministry, portraying specific women of the Bible. Gerrie dresses in period costume and assumes the role of a Biblical character to tell first-person stories of faith.

You can contact Gerrie through her website.
www.gerriemills.com

Gerrie Hyman Mills

Holy Chutzpah!